D0247975

Contents

ALCOHOLISM

The Family Guide

Samantha
Harrington-Lowe

Need
– 2 –
Know

TULLAMORE SEP 2023 WITHDRAWN

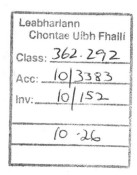

Leabharlann
    Chontae Uíbh Fhailí
Class: 362.292
Acc: 10|3383
Inv: 10|152

10-26

First published in Great Britain in 2008 by
Need2Know
Remus House
Coltsfoot Drive
Peterborough
PE2 9JX
Telephone 01733 898103
Fax 01733 313524
www.need2knowbooks.co.uk

Need2Know is an imprint of Forward Press Ltd.
www.forwardpress.co.uk
All Rights Reserved
© Samantha Harrington-Lowe 2008
Cartoons: Mark Bayliss
SB ISBN 978-1-86144-050-1

Introduction

Alcoholism, or as it's also known, alcohol dependency, and other related drinking problems are at an all time high in the UK, and it's the world's number one drug problem. One of the most potentially damaging drugs existing, it's legal to purchase and consume, advertised widely on the mind-boggling variety of media available to the consumer, and to be found in most households the nation over. Its use ranges from the measured intake of the wine connoisseur to the desperate consumption by the street dweller of cheap cider or worse.

Being an alcoholic conjures up images of a huddle of desperados on street corners or lurking outside drop-in centres. But the truth is far more disturbing. There are hundreds of thousands of people in the UK today who have a serious drink problem. The problems range from acute stage alcoholism to binge drinking, with much in between; and irresponsible drinking amongst young people is frighteningly high. Children and families suffer at the hands of the alcoholic and domestic violence is inextricably linked with its use. Its misuse also fills up the A&E departments of hospitals – clearly it is an increasing problem, rather than the reverse.

The chances are that you will definitely know at least one or two people who have a drink issue, maybe more. And one of those people could be you.

Why people become alcoholics is a hard issue to clarify. Research seems to emphasise that there is a hereditary genetic weakness that can lead to alcohol dependency, but growing up with alcoholic parents, or just plain bad luck, can also contribute hugely to the cause.

The biggest hurdle when tackling an alcohol issue is coming to terms with the fact that you have a problem. Until that time, there is little anyone can do to help you, and you will have skirted round this repeatedly, making excuses, pretending to yourself and those close to you that everything is okay. In fact, the alcoholic is generally a highly skilled liar and it will often take some kind of crisis to really open their eyes. If you're the person living with an alcoholic, knowing this is paramount. You, yourself, can do nothing to change them; it has to come from them.

'Between 1991 and 2005, deaths directly attributed to alcohol almost doubled.'
BMJ. December 2007.

But if it's you with the problem and you've picked up this book, you have made that frightening and so important first step by acknowledging there is an issue. Well done. It really is a massive move forward.

If it's someone else you're worried about, then this book should help you to understand the condition better, and to look at your options more clearly. It's an illness and needs to be understood as such.

Dealing with an alcohol problem is never going to be easy, and this book is not designed to assist in isolation with your journey. Research proves that giving up is almost impossible without some kind of outside support, and I can't recommend enough that anyone dealing with this seeks counselling and medical advice as soon as possible. But this book is here to guide and help out where possible; to highlight support options, impart general medical information and hopefully shine a light on to the path you are starting to tread.

It's time to take control and start living your life again, free of the suffocating and potentially fatal restrictions of alcohol dependence. Let's get that freedom back again and stop the suffering caused to those addicted and to those who love the sufferer. I hope I can help you along the way, however this is affecting you.

Disclaimer

This book is for general information about alcoholism. It is not intended to replace professional medical advice. It can be used alongside medical advice, but anyone with concerns is strongly advised to consult their GP.

Whilst every care has been taken to validate the contents of this guide up to the time of going to press, the author advises that she does not claim medical qualifications. Readers should seek advice from a qualified medical practitioner before undertaking any particular course of treatment.

Chapter One

What is Alcoholism?

The facts

Firstly, let's look at the clear definition of alcoholism. True alcoholism is a disease. It's not something the sufferer chooses, and stopping, for them, is not simply a case of saying 'No, thanks'. It is a compulsive and progressive disease that can affect physical and mental health. Not only that, it causes problems with family, friends and work.

It is not necessarily the person who had a heavy night on Saturday and overdid things. The term 'alcoholic' is often used loosely, but the difference between the alcoholic and someone who enjoys a drink and even occasionally goes overboard, is clearly defined.

Also known as 'Alcohol Dependence Syndrome', alcoholism is clearly defined in four ways: cravings, no control, physical reliance and capacity.

Cravings

It's probably fair to say that the majority of us have at some point thought 'I really fancy a glass of wine, or a cold beer'. This is not what we mean by craving. Craving for the alcoholic is a very different matter. It's a strong compulsion, a driving need to consume alcohol that overtakes everything else going on until the compulsion is satisfied.

No control

Loss of control in this sense doesn't mean getting so drunk you can't stand up. It means the complete inability to stop drinking once you have begun. The alcoholic will find it almost impossible to regulate moderate drinking, and almost certainly be incapable of switching to a soft drink, for example. They will have no control over their intake, only to keep drinking compulsively. Running out of booze is just not an option.

Physical reliance

Just the same as the drug addict, the alcoholic's body will become reliant on their intake, and the alcoholic will need to keep those levels topped up to stop feeling ill – often just to feel normal. Withdrawal symptoms when giving up heavy and prolonged drinking include nausea, sweating, paranoia, shakiness, and anxiety. In some cases seizures and hallucinations are possible and finally, in the most extreme cases, full blown delirium tremens – or the DTs as they're commonly known. Often, the milder symptoms can be a regular daily occurrence upon waking, only relieved by drinking alcohol or by taking calming drugs such as beta blockers or diazepam.

Capacity

The more you drink, the more you need to drink. Aside from the physical dependence of drinking just to stop feeling dreadful, the alcoholic is also seeking that elusive 'high' - and as time goes by, the quantity of alcohol needed to achieve that increases. The alcoholic is not fussy either. They will drink whatever is available – whether it's cooking wine that's been on the side for days, or cheap cider. It's not about having a discerning palate, it's about the end result.

So you can see why this is a difficult situation for the alcoholic. It's not a simple case of drinking less or taking it easy, it's far more complex. It's more important to them than eating and will take first place over children and family, work, friends or even the alcoholic's own well-being. It's all-consuming.

Other drink-related conditions

Alcoholism in its most classic form is a debilitating disease. But there are other forms of drink problems.

Binge drinking

Very popular amongst younger people and teenagers, particularly women, and often used by nervous or shy people to boost their confidence. The binge drinker is usually a habitually moderate drinker during the week, but goes on wild benders at the weekend. The physical strain this places on the liver and body makes it a dangerous sport anyway, but it can also lead to memory loss, related behavioural problems such as fighting or casual sex (often unprotected), lost weekends and huge financial outlay. It also leaves the drinker open to spiking, as they lose control of what's going on around them. (See the case study on page 39 for more information on binge drinking.)

Underage drinking

This is a worrying upward trend. Youngsters are drinking more and more, their sophisticated outward appearance making it possible to purchase alcohol in shops and in pubs. The rise of the 'alcopop' has made the products more palatable to younger taste buds and children as young as nine or 10 have been reported turning up for school drunk.

Foetal Alcohol Syndrome

The odd glass of wine isn't going to do too much harm, but there are a disturbing number of women who drink regularly and continuously through their pregnancy and this can lead to Foetal Alcohol Syndrome. Heavy continuous drinking or binge drinking throughout pregnancy can have a profound effect on unborn children, leading to premature and underweight babies, with skeletal and neurological weaknesses. (See chapter 6 for further information.)

Alcoholic poisoning

Seen mostly in the binge drinker, alcoholic poisoning is no joke. Fast drinking slows down reactions and as the body becomes incapable of processing the intake, the brain stops being able to govern the body properly. Signs of alcoholic poisoning can include vomiting, clammy skin, unconsciousness, wetting oneself, slow and laboured breathing – and the only course of action here is to place the drinker in the recovery position and call 999 fast.

'The alcoholic is at the mercy of a far greater drive to destruction. It may seem like self-indulgence to the observer, but the alcoholic needs treatment in the same way as any other sufferer from disease.'

Dual addiction

It's very often the case that alcoholism goes hand in hand with some kind of other addiction. Sometimes this is simply nicotine, but very often alcohol abuse is seen with heavy cocaine, amphetamine and other drug use. The effects of alcohol can intensify the high produced by these drugs, particularly cocaine, and it would be wise for the user to treat both the alcohol and the drug problem simultaneously. Giving up one at a time will only lead to downfall.

Spotting the difference

The alcoholic will often display many of these behavioural patterns. But don't be confused. These conditions – whilst being a definite cause for concern – are largely self-inflicted, and if daily, compulsive drinking is absent where some of these other behavioural patterns are seen, then you are probably not looking at an alcoholic. The alcoholic is at the mercy of a far greater drive to destruction.

It may seem like self-indulgence to the observer, but the alcoholic needs treatment in the same way as any other sufferer from disease.

There are a minority of people who can recover without help. But these are few and far between, as it's not simply a case of will power. The majority of alcoholic individuals will need help, support and treatment to recover from their disease.

Is it inherited?

The short answer is yes, it is believed to be hereditary. There is a propensity for the children of alcoholics to become vulnerable to the same condition as their parent. But it's not a foregone conclusion and there are 'risk factors' involved which can have a marked effect on the potentiality of following in an alcoholic's footsteps.

It's not just a case of being 'in the blood'. Environmental issues will affect the outcome too, as will peer group behaviour and the availability of alcohol – in fact all these things can contribute. Many children of alcoholics enjoy a sensible relationship with drink.

If you had alcoholic parents, it's a wise precaution to be aware of the higher chances of your own susceptibility, but be careful to draw the line between being aware and living in fear. There is no need to create a self-fulfilling prophecy, just be careful. There is more about this issue in chapter 3.

The end result

Without treatment, alcoholism is a slow, degenerative disease which is, ultimately, potentially fatal. And it's not a nice way to go. The good news is that it's treatable, providing the alcoholic is prepared to face up to the problem. Recovering is difficult, and the only way to proceed is total abstinence. There is no such thing as the 'odd drink' for an alcoholic.

The table overleaf shows the number of alcohol-related deaths in the UK from 1991-2006.

'It's not just a case of being "in the blood". Environmental issues will affect the outcome too, as will peer group behaviour and the availability of alcohol – in fact all these things can contribute.'

Year	Males rate per 100,000 population	Females rate per 100,000 population
1991	9.1	5.0
1992	9.0	4.6
1993	9.1	4.8
1994	10.0	5.2
1995	11.2	5.8
1996	12.1	6.1
1997	13.4	6.6
1998	14.4	6.8
1999	14.9	7.3
2000	15.2	7.4
2001	16.5	7.8
2002	16.8	7.9
2003	17.8	8.1
2004	17.6	8.3
2005	17.9	8.3
2006	18.3	8.8

Data taken from Office for National Statistics, www.statistics.gov.uk.

Summing Up

There is a big difference between the occasional and social drinker – and even the binge drinker – and the alcoholic or alcohol dependant. The alcoholic feels like they just cannot live without the drink. It consumes them from the minute they open their eyes until they close them again at the end of the day, and they will move heaven and earth to get hold of alcohol if there's none around. Often they will be in a mess physically too, unable to eat properly or shaking uncontrollably until they start drinking again. Liver damage, heart disease, coronary attack, confused or anxious mental state and risk of cancer are all dangers for the chronic alcoholic. But the good news is that giving up will reverse a lot of the damage.

Once the alcoholic has wrestled with their demons and kicked the habit, however, they will not be able to drink again. There is no 'odd glass of wine' for the alcoholic.

Chapter Two

Spotting the Problem

The signs

Alcoholism as a condition means that the desire for booze is stronger than pretty much anything else in your life. Alcohol dependency, realistically, is next down the scale, as this may involve a reliance on drink to cope with situations, such as anxiety or shyness. And there's alcohol abuse, which is the category in which to place binge drinking and so on. If you think you are an alcoholic or alcohol abuser, or you suspect someone else might be, there are some fairly standard signs to look out for.

Are you an alcoholic?

Is it you you're worried about? Take the quick quiz overleaf and think carefully about your answers. Simply tick all those questions you can answer with a *yes* and tot up the total below.

The questions apply to the subject, but can easily be applied to someone you know if it's not yourself you're concerned about.

'Without treatment, alcoholism is a slow, degenerative disease which is, ultimately, potentially fatal. And it's not a nice way to go. The good news is that it's treatable, providing the alcoholic is prepared to face up to the problem. Recovering is difficult, and the only way to proceed is total abstinence.'

Are you an alcoholic?

Do you drink to escape from problems?

Do you drink because you are shy?

Do you drink alone?

Do you often have six or more units at one time?

Do you ever feel remorseful or embarrassed after drinking?

Have you ever had a loss of memory as a result of drinking?

Have you missed work because of drinking?

Is drinking affecting your home life?

Have you got a bit of a reputation as a drinker?

Does drinking make you thoughtless about your family?

Do you hide your drinking from other people?

Has drinking made you lose interest in your career?

Do you crave a drink at a certain time each day?

Do you want a drink the following morning?

Has a doctor or clinician ever treated you for drinking?

Have you ever been to a hospital (including A&E) or institution because of drinking?

In the last year has a relative or friend, or a doctor or other health worker been concerned about your drinking or suggested you cut down?

Answering *yes* to more than three or four of these questions indicates a definite alcohol problem. The more *yeses*, the bigger the issue. You may feel that you are in control of your drinking, but these questions are carefully constructed to highlight problem areas. It's easy to drift along, thinking that everything is okay, and hiding from the issue. But if you've got a few *yeses* above, you need to look more closely.

Is someone you know an alcoholic?

Problem drinking is far more common than you think. Whether it's alcohol abuse, alcohol dependence or alcoholism, the chances are you know at least one person either at home, at work or in your social circle who has a drink problem. It could even be one of your parents.

The quiz below is based on one devised by Al Anon, a family support body set up to help those who are affected by someone else's drinking. If you're not sure whether the person you know has a problem or not, this can give a good indication.

Do you have a parent, close friend or relative whose drinking upsets you?

Do you cover up your real feelings by pretending you don't care?

Does it seem like every holiday is spoiled because of drinking?

Do you tell lies to cover up for someone else's drinking or what's happening in your home?

Do you stay out of the house as much as possible because you hate it there?

Are you afraid to upset someone for fear it will set off a drinking bout?

Do you feel nobody really loves you or cares what happens to you?

Are you afraid or embarrassed to bring your friends home?

Do you think the drinker's behaviour is caused by you, other members of your family, friends or rotten breaks in life?

Do you believe no one could possibly understand how you feel?

Do you have money problems because of someone else's drinking?

Are meal times frequently delayed because of the drinker?

Have you considered calling the police because of drinking behaviour?

Have you refused dates out of fear or anxiety?

Do you think that if the drinker stopped drinking, your other problems would be solved?

Answering yes to more than two or three questions definitely indicates cause for concern.

For further information, contact Al-Anon Family Groups Headquarters, 1600 Corporate Landing Parkway, Virginia Beach, VA 23454-5617, USA. Tel: (757) 563-1600, www.al-anon.org.

It may be that you feel helpless in the face of someone else's drinking problem, and I'm not going to lie to you – you are never going to find it easy to cope. It's up to the drinker to face his or her problem and deal with it. But it's not all doom and gloom. There are many, many support groups for those affected by alcohol abusers and it's important to realise you are not alone.

'The chances are you know at least one person either at home, at work or in your social circle who has a drink problem.'

The help list at the back of the book looks in greater detail at the support groups and help options available, both online and in person. Research shows that getting some help and advice on coping makes the issue easier to deal with, and the most important thing is to find an outlet to talk to others about what you're going through. It will make a huge difference in the way you cope.

Affecting your life?

Alcohol problems can affect the lives not just of those addicted, but those around them too – often more so, in actual fact. It's very hard to watch a dearly loved friend or family member destroying himself or herself in this way. Or perhaps you work with someone who is making life difficult – leaving you to cover for their lateness, long lunches or sloppy work.

What is harder to understand is the behaviour that goes with it: lying to cover the habit, putting everything else further down the list of priorities, and, of course, the drunken behaviour itself.

Out and about, you will notice they generally drink much more and much faster than anyone else, behave inappropriately in social situations and can often become argumentative and aggressive or withdrawn and tearful. You will also notice their capacity for drink is way beyond anyone else's – they can drink an awful lot and still stand up.

At home it may be different, a bit less noisy perhaps. But alcoholics can be difficult to live with – again, drinking can cause arguments, violence and irrational behaviour. It's not much fun, especially if it's your mum or dad.

And if it's you who has the problem, deep down you're quite possibly aware of all this. It makes you feel pretty worthless, which in turn can make giving up even harder.

The important thing to remember here, whether you're the one drinking or the one affected by it, is that it is not deliberate. It's hard not to take it all personally, but alcoholism is an illness and needs to be treated as such.

'Whether the alcoholic is at home or out and about, their behaviour will differ clearly from other people's and can often be unpleasant, difficult or embarrassing.'

Summing Up

Alcohol-related problems are far more common than a lot of people realise and it could easily be you that has the problem without even knowing it.

Taking the quizzes will certainly help to highlight any issues, and may prove to be a wake up call, whatever your situation.

The good news is that coming to the realisation that there is an alcohol problem to address is often the biggest step. Denial and avoidance are key in this insidious illness, and facing it will definitely be a positive move.

Chapter Three

Alcoholism and the Family

Is it hereditary?

It's true to say that alcoholism can be hereditary. If you're a person with an alcoholic parent then you already run a high risk of developing the condition yourself. However, this is not to say that it will definitely happen, nor is it a reason to avoid the issue. Just because you have a greater chance of being an alcoholic does not mean it will necessarily be your legacy.

It does mean, however, that you will need to be more self aware than other people. There are three main factors you will need to keep in mind.

Heredity

Alcoholism tends to run in families and genetics are partly responsible. Research sourced from The National Institute of Alcohol Abuse and Alcoholism (NIAAA) *Alcohol Alert* shows that studies are being carried out to seek out and understand those genes that make a person predisposed towards alcoholism. The current popular opinion is that it's this genetic anomaly, coupled with the environment and learnt behaviour that creates the alcoholic. It's not necessarily just 'in the blood'.

Research sourced from NIAAA *Alcohol Alert* also shows that identical twins who are the offspring of an alcoholic parent and who live separately without knowledge of each other have both developed alcoholism independently. This has also been proven with adopted children who have alcoholic biological parents but normal adoptive parents and have gone on to develop alcohol–related conditions themselves.

It is a fact, unfortunately, that the genetic odds are stacked against the children of alcoholics.

'If you're a person with an alcoholic parent then you already run a high risk of developing the condition yourself.'

Environment

It's not just about your genes though. Environmental issues can play a huge part in developing a drink problem. Children of alcoholics are known to have higher anxiety levels, live with pervasive tension and disorder at home, and tend to achieve less well at school than they should. An unhappy childhood can have a great influence over future behaviour.

Habit

Finally of course there is learnt behaviour and bad habits. If all a child has ever known is habitual heavy drinking and unreasonable behaviour, it's going to be hard for them to realise that's not the normal way to live. Adjusting to life outside the family will be hard and it will be a challenge not to fall into the habits seen at home.

In summary, all three aspects contribute to the problem, and if you're a child of an alcoholic, the basic fact is you're going to have to be doubly careful not to follow that path.

Case study - Jim[*]

Jim is now in his late thirties and is an alcoholic. His mother was an alcoholic too and he says growing up in that situation has directly contributed to his own addiction.

'When I was younger, I only really remember how much she used to drink,' he says. 'Every day I would come home from school and it wasn't like, would she be drunk, it was like, *how* drunk will she be. My father hated it, but didn't know what to do. I can see now, looking back, that he felt completely helpless and in the seventies there was less awareness about alcohol abuse than there is now. So he'd either be furious, trying to stop her, or he'd just not be there. I preferred it when he didn't come home to be honest; I hated the arguments, they used to make me feel really sick, listening upstairs.'

Jim's mother used to blame him and his younger sister repeatedly for the problems at home. But rather than admit to there being a problem with her drinking, she used to look for different excuses.

'She'd often be crying, pointing the finger at us. Completely drunk of course, she would say over and over how unhappy she was, and that it was because of us, because of my father, because of everything basically, except the alcohol. It was a real case of her feeling like "I could have been someone", except that all the reasons for her not being whatever she wanted to be were in her head. She could have done whatever she liked really, except she was mashed every day of the week.

'I could never bring home friends, it was too embarrassing. I mean, I didn't care too much when I was younger, but when I got to my teenage years, I couldn't bear my friends seeing what my home life was like. I was sure they talked about me at school so I avoided ever discussing it with anyone. I used to avoid going home for as long as possible every day, and I couldn't stand the mess everywhere. By the time I got to about 11 she'd stopped bothering to try and make dinner for us or whatever, so I used to sort that stuff out with my younger sister. Sometimes it was even impossible to do homework – she'd appear in your bedroom, shouting and crying. It was a nightmare. I wanted so much to get away.'

Jim says that from an early age, his mother encouraged him to try drinking at home, even buying alcohol that she knew he and his sister would like. He feels this has contributed directly to his own addiction.

'In those days before alcopops, she would get in stuff like Dubonnet, which was really sweet, and mix it with lemonade for us. I can see now that she was looking for someone to share her complicity so she wouldn't feel so guilty, but looking back, it makes me so very, very angry. I don't think I ever stood a chance, to be honest. Fancy giving kids alcohol just to make yourself feel better about your own drinking. That's how strong the addiction can be, how unrealistic and selfish it makes you.'

Jim's mother died when he was just 17, which he says was sad but a bit of a relief too. She had very brief periods of not drinking – pretty much when her body gave out a couple of times and she ended up in hospital. But her heart was never in it and she went back to the drink after a very short period of time. The big difference between Jim and his mother though, is that Jim knows he has a problem and is trying his best to face it. He has admitted that he has no children because he didn't want to put them through what he and his sister went through, which is terribly sad. But he seems quite pragmatic about this.

'In a weird way I now have more sympathy for her because I know how she felt,' he says. 'I didn't really notice it, my drinking, until suddenly I realised my life was falling apart. I run a B&B and bar and do the breakfasts. I'm in the hotel all day, so I am not at a desk under anyone's eye. I was finding that I was getting to around lunchtime and starting on the booze. I suffer from anxiety and found drinking helps to take the edge off that, so it was getting earlier and earlier each day. Then I realised that actually, if I didn't have a drink first thing in the morning, I wouldn't be able to get through the day without being really shaky. Suddenly I knew it - I had the same bloody problem and I hadn't even seen it coming. I can't sleep properly, I can't eat first thing until I've had a few beers or I throw up, and my bowel movements are best not talked about, frankly.'

Jim is now working towards quitting, although he freely admits it scares the life out of him, and he's finding it really hard.

'You have no idea what it's like unless you can stand in my shoes. I am also massively agoraphobic which has either been caused by my drinking or made worse by it, I'm not sure. But I find even going to the shops terrifying. Last year I worked up enough courage to have my first holiday away from the B&B for a few years and had to pretty much get blotto to even tackle it. Then I found we were staying in a place where the nearest shop that sold alcohol was miles away.

'I was up, 5am, pacing around and made my wife drive me to sit outside the shop, waiting for it to open. I was shaking and terrified until the doors opened and I went in to get the stuff. I didn't even drink much when I could get my hands on it, but the fact of not having any was the most frightening thing I've ever been through. I was weeping in the car, shaking uncontrollably, absolutely petrified. I knew it was the end of the line and since we came back I've been working at sorting it out. But I'll be the first to tell you, I'm scared to death.'

Jim is working at cutting down before giving up, believing that this will soften the blow when he finally stops. His aim is to get to the afternoon before having that first drink, but it's hard. He often backslides and needs to start again, cutting back gradually.

'I need to put some kind of limit on this,' he confesses, 'because it's dragging on a bit. I guess I'm putting it off but I really am trying, and at least I'm making a difference, however small. I've got a buddy I can talk to when I feel bad and the doc has given me some beta-blockers for anxiety. But I can't go to AA until I quit and I am just too scared to give up totally just yet. I will get there though, I am determined not to do the same thing as my mother.'

*Names have been changed to protect identities.

Living with an alcoholic

Alcoholism is a family disease, and anyone who has not lived with an alcohol abuser will find it hard to understand what it's like. As Jim's experience demonstrates, drinking alcohol alters behaviour and this can be happening on a daily basis, changing the personality of the drinker. It's like watching the person you know morph into someone else.

Social embarrassment is high on the list of worries – drinkers will often let themselves down by behaving badly and social invites will dry up. Holidays are ruined by unacceptable behaviour and rows, and home life becomes tense and unhappy.

Bodily functions are affected, as are sleep patterns, and it's not unusual for sleepwalking, coupled with urinating in the wrong places, to be common. Housework and homemaking go out of the window. Work is normally affected, with the drinker even losing jobs and there is generally a financial burden. But most of all, the drain is emotional.

It's also a sad fact that abuse, both sexual and physical, is a high risk factor in alcoholic homes – this can be aimed at children or partners. Aggression and violence in general are familiar occurrences, with a vast percentage of domestic violence cases linked to alcohol abuse.

Alcoholics will often blame everyone but themselves for the problems they create, and until there is some kind of crisis – usually a sort of breakdown on the part of the alcoholic – the greatest issue will be denial. Drinkers hide evidence of their intake and lie continuously about their control over the matter. As Jim's experience showed, those living with such a person will feel completely helpless.

The hot bath

Someone once gave me a great analogy for living with an alcoholic. Imagine if you got into a bath that was far too hot for you. You'd get straight back out, because it's not comfortable, it hurts. But if you get into a cooler bath and gradually add hot water until it's the same temperature, the chances are you'd be able to stand it, and you'd stay put. It's the same here. Often the drinking problem starts small and grows, until you are living with a completely unacceptable lifestyle that you wouldn't have dreamt of in a million years, and would never put up with if you'd known it to be like this at the start. The trouble with living with alcoholism is that you don't detect the creeping heat until suddenly, without noticing, you're sitting in a bath of water that's far too hot.

It's a very difficult and damaging situation to live with and this is why support groups help enormously – you will find understanding amongst others who live with similar situations.

'It's a phrase often used, and reflects the situation accurately... Alcoholism is a family disease. Whoever is suffering from the condition will affect all those around them, causing turmoil and friction. It becomes everyone's problem.'

Why me?

It's very important to understand that alcoholics don't develop a problem with alcohol because it's fun, and more often than not, the alcoholic is an unhappy person because of it. It's a complex condition affected by genetics, environment and heredity. Alcoholics don't usually drink to enjoy life; they drink because they can't help it.

The people living and working with them suffer too, and especially if you're a child living in this situation it's really hard not to wonder if it's your fault. Perhaps if you did something differently, things would change?

Stop right there.

The drinker is the only person that can make a difference to their drinking patterns. You have to try really hard not to take the behaviour personally and not feel it's your place to change things. It isn't, and it's absolutely not your fault. Come to that, it's not the alcoholic's either, although it will feel very much like it is. Blaming either yourself or them will not help. The best thing you can do for yourself is get some support from people who understand your situation, and be there for the alcoholic when finally they are ready to change their life.

Enabling patterns

Although it is very important to realise that you are not the cause of someone's alcoholism, sometimes, without realising it, you can be living with an alcoholic and actually helping them to continue their self abuse. Your actions are well intentioned, usually meant to help or support, but you could be enabling the continuation of the problem.

Have you ever called in 'sick' for the person when they've been too hung over to work? Or made excuses for their drinking? Perhaps you've lent them money or paid their bills for them. Maybe you've even tried drinking with them to create some kind of solidarity. Or have you threatened to leave, more than once, but stayed put? Any of these actions will do nothing but help to enable the drinker, and they need to be looked at carefully.

Enabling patterns tend to fall into three main categories.

The saviour

The saviour is the one who rushes to help the alcoholic and works to maintain some semblance of normality. They will catch the drunk when they fall, put a duvet over them when they pass out on the floor, clear up their mess and cheerfully make breakfast in the morning without a word. They will lie to cover the alcoholic's actions. They strive to make everything okay and in doing so protect the drinker from the consequences of his or her actions. These heroic efforts mean that the drinker can go about feeling that it's all okay. There is little motivation to get help.

The victim

Seeking to lay a massive guilt trip on the alcoholic, the victim's *modus operandi* is to try and shame the drinker into changing. The victim will feel the burden of the situation very heavily and will often be in tears, making heartfelt whispered telephone calls to friends for support, but saying little to the alcoholic. Usually the victim will become withdrawn and depressed, and this behavioural pattern realistically only gives the alcoholic something to focus on other than him or herself. Frequently they become irritated by the victim's martyr-like behaviour and will seek to punish, causing arguments and making the victim even worse. It's a destructive downward spiral that does nothing except distract everyone from the real problem.

The aggravator

The aggravator is the angry one of the three. Furious at the alcoholic's behaviour, they will shout, get angry over the drinker's actions, belittle and berate them. The aggravator tries to change behaviour by threatening to leave or by using a constant stream of anger and resentment, hoping in the end it will get through. The house is filled with rage and arguments and the aggravator will often involve other people to gain extra support. This course of action usually only serves to drive the drinking further underground. Finding the strength or headspace to stop when there is rage all around is hard, and again, this fighting is just another distraction from the real issues.

Of course children's behaviour rarely falls into these patterns and their reactions are likely to be more instinctive. They hide, plead or run. They will often find themselves blamed for the problem, as the alcoholic looks for yet another excuse.

Breaking the cycle

It's not all hopeless though, I promise. Although, as I've said, you cannot realistically change the alcoholic, you can do something to help. And the best thing to do is nothing.

Not reacting is the most positive step you can take within your limited options. If they're looking for an argument, don't rise to it; if they can't get out of bed in the morning, don't let it affect your own routine. If you stop making it your problem, it's only theirs to deal with and eventually having to face it alone will generate a more willing attitude on their part to accept reality. Any kind of collusion, whether it's mopping up after them or giving them something else to think about, such as an argument, will only detract from their self analysis. Leave them to get on with it.

Summing Up

It's a phrase often used, and reflects the situation accurately... Alcoholism is a family disease. Whoever is suffering from the condition will affect all those around them, causing turmoil and friction. It becomes everyone's problem – just remember Jim's experiences.

Growing up with that can have a profound effect on a person, so it's no wonder the children of alcoholics are changed by this. The study of genetics and the predisposition towards inheriting the illness has also shown that there really is a link, but by no means should this be taken to mean it's a foregone conclusion. If you're living with the alcoholic, try not to assume those roles that make it hard for them to face their problems. And if it's you with the drink problem, try to see what's going on around you – you're probably not much fun to be with!

Anyone who's reading this book and has got this far is highly likely to be in a receptive state – you wouldn't be reading this otherwise! You are ready to take control of the situation and break those habits. And, therefore, you stand a good chance of finding an alternative to the destructive path of alcoholism.

Chapter Four

Teenage and Underage Drinking

Younger drinkers

Alcoholism is normally regarded as an older person's problem, not usually seen in anyone younger than 30. Whilst it may take a few years for true alcoholism to become a full-blown condition, this does not mean that alcohol problems are confined to the older generation.

Teenage drinking is well-documented in the press these days; the rise of binge drinking amongst young people and the proliferation of underage drinking make for shocking headlines. But the problem is real and the headlines only show part of the issue.

A recent BBC survey has discovered that children as young as six have been admitted to hospital after binge drinking on alcopops. The Corporation's study of 50 A&E departments discovered that in one unit alone, as many as 100 drunken children one week were seen, and 70% of staff believe that child admissions are consistently getting younger.

'A recent BBC survey has discovered that children as young as six have been admitted to hospital after binge drinking on alcopops.'

Having a good time?

There is sometimes an attitude amongst young people that the definition of having a good night out is getting completely wasted. Of course this is not the case for all youngsters, but the rise in teenage and even younger drinkers shows an alarming upward trend in binge drinking. See the table overleaf for statistics.

How much are young people drinking?

Mean alcohol consumption (in units) of pupils who had drunk in the last seven days, by gender and age, 1990 to 2006 (England)

	1990	1992	1994	1996	1998	2000	2001	2002	2003	2004	2005	2006
All pupils All ages	5.3	6.0	6.4	8.4	9.9	10.4	9.8	10.6	9.5	10.7	10.5	11.4
Aged 11-13	-	3.4	4.1	5.5	6.3	6.4	5.6	6.8	7.1	7.8	8.2	10.1
Aged 14	-	4.7	6.1	7.7	9.9	9.8	9.6	10.3	9.0	9.9	10.3	10.9
Aged 15	-	8.1	7.7	10.4	11.5	12.9	12.3	13.0	11.3	12.9	11.8	12.3
Boys All Ages	5.7	7.0	7.4	9.7	11.3	11.7	10.6	11.5	10.5	11.3	11.5	12.3
Aged 11-13	-	3.6	5.2	7.1	6.2	8.3	5.5	7.3	7.7	8.1	8.6	11.9
Aged 14	-	5.3	6.7	7.3	12.3	9.5	10.0	10.7	9.4	10.1	11.1	10.1
Aged 15	-	9.6	8.8	12.9	12.9	14.5	13.8	14.3	12.9	13.9	13.1	13.9
Girls All ages	4.7	4.7	5.4	7.0	8.4	9.1	8.0	9.6	8.5	10.2	9.5	10.5
Aged 11-13	-	3.1	3.0	4.0	6.4	4.6	5.7	6.3	6.4	7.3	7.9	8.4
Aged 14	-	3.8	5.5	8.2	8.1	10.1	9.3	10.0	8.7	9.7	9.5	11.7
Aged 15	-	6.0	6.6	8.0	9.7	11.2	10.7	11.4	9.6	12.1	10.5	10.9

Source: Smoking, drinking and drug use among young people in England in 2006. The Information Centre for Health and Social Care. 2007.

It's not just the health issues that matter, although of course this is something to think about carefully. Drinking irresponsibly can place young people in risky situations, ranging from having a drink spiked and being raped, to getting arrested for throwing up in the street. Seriously, vomiting or urinating in the street is classed as anti-social behaviour and can get you an £80 fine.

For girls, the biggest issue is usually their physical vulnerability. Less able physically to consume vast amounts of alcohol, girls are more likely to be ill, but they're also twice as likely to be assaulted sexually. According to the website Know Your Limits, one in three reported rapes happen when the victim has been drinking. Spiking drinks is on the up, and if you're out of control in the first place it's much more likely to happen to you.

It's worth remembering the number one date rape drug is alcohol.

It's not just girls that can be taken advantage of though. Boys can get beaten up, mugged or attacked when under the influence. And of course boys can also be drugged and raped as well. Rapists are not confined to the heterosexual world but can be homosexual too.

For boys, the daredevil inside every man is often released after several pints. Drinking too much can make you feel invincible. Stunt behaviour like climbing walls, hoardings and scaffolding might seem like a bit of boyish fun when you're smashed, but smashed is what you'll be when you hit the ground. You're not Superman. According to Know Your Limits 70% of all A&E admissions between the hours of midnight and 5am are alcohol-related and this includes accidents.

Accidents happen on the streets too, and when you're drunk, you wobble. Fact. What is also a fact is that eight out of 10 pedestrians knocked down and killed on Friday or Saturday nights have been drinking. You might think you're fine, but you're not. Watch where you're walking.

And something for both sexes to think about. Drinking can lead to irresponsible sexual activity, leading to unwanted pregnancies and STIs. Use a condom – if sex can actually happen that is. 'Brewer's Droop' is so named because too much alcohol will definitely affect performance, so if you have a special night in mind, a skinful at the pub beforehand is not going to help.

'Stunt behaviour like climbing walls, hoardings and scaffolding might seem like a bit of boyish fun when you're smashed, but smashed is what you'll be when you hit the ground.'

The dangerous alcopop

This is the bad guy of the teenage and underage drinking world. Prettily packaged and sugary sweet like fruity fizzy drinks, the alcopop is, without a doubt, aimed specifically at a younger market. Alcopops were launched onto the UK drinks market around the mid 90s, with drinks like Two Dogs and Hooch the first in line. Marketed as alcoholic lemonade, their sugary sharpness was an instant success and paved the way for hundreds of imitators.

These days the alcopop is a far more sophisticated blend of taste, packaging and marketing. The most recent kafuffle has been about the vodka-based 'aphrodisiac' drink Roxxoff, with a herbal libido enhancer. With the obvious implication being that this drink will improve your sex life, it's the latest in a long line of carefully placed products aimed with deadly accuracy at the young drinker. Hilarious really, as too much booze definitely has the opposite effect on your sexual performance.

The alcopop has come under considerable criticism by watchdogs and the Portman Group in particular. The Portman Group is a collective that was formed in 1989 by the UK's leading alcohol producers, as it says on their website 'to promote sensible drinking; to help prevent alcohol misuse; and to foster a balanced understanding of alcohol-related issues.' (See www.portman-group.org.uk.) They have some real issues with the way alcopops are marketed.

The thing to remember with alcopops is that although they taste delicious and the advertising makes them look cool, don't be fooled by the booze companies. These pops will make you drunk just like any other alcoholic drink and will lead to just the same problems as anything else. No good for your teeth either, or your breath, come to that!

Is it your child?

Having a youngster or teenager that you suspect is drinking too much or drinking underage is an uncomfortable predicament. But how do you tackle it?

Talking to them is the first port of call. I don't mean shouting and arguing, but calmly sitting down and explaining the dangers of drinking and the positive aspects of a healthier lifestyle. Plan what you're going to say first and then

'Children learn by example a lot of the time so teaching them a sensible attitude starts with your own behaviour. Don't let them see you falling about drunk, or drinking heavily all the time. It's not good for them, and it's not good for you either.'

open it like a conversation rather than a lecture. Ask them to give their thoughts and opinions, and make sure you're prepared for any questions or rebuttals. Most importantly, however, you should stay calm.

Children learn by example a lot of the time so teaching them a sensible attitude starts with your own behaviour. Don't let them see you falling about drunk or drinking heavily all the time. It's not good for them, and it's not good for you either.

Drink responsibly and make sure you're up-to-date on all the information relating to the dangers of alcohol, such as the physical effects, spiking and date rape and so on. Your offspring will be much more likely to respect your advice if you know what you're talking about.

Above all, be realistic. Teenagers have always experimented with alcohol and today's generation is no different. You may well remember indulging yourself. Try and advise your child how to say no thanks without losing face, such as 'I don't like it', 'It's too high in calories' or 'It makes me sick'.

Be down-to-earth too and give them practical advice such as how to stay safe, how to watch out for being spiked or mugged, and let them know that you'll always be there at the end of the phone if things really go wrong. The last thing you want is for them to be afraid to call home – who knows what could happen then.

A good night out

When having a night at the club or pub with your mates – whether you're of legal drinking age or not – there are some golden rules to ensure you have a great night out that you'll remember.

Eat first

Food slows down the way alcohol gets into your bloodstream. Not only that but you'll feel better the next day!

Avoid rounds

Don't get sucked into drinking in rounds, which often means ending up drinking more and faster to match the group's pace.

Opt out occasionally

A great way to lessen your intake is to vary your drinks – try alternating alcoholic drinks with non-alcoholic drinks. Hydrating your body and laying off the alcohol will not only make you happier the next morning, it'll improve your night out in the first place. You'll feel more energised and will definitely be a better dancer!

Ignore peer pressure

You might find your friends or drinking buddies are hassling you to join in. Real mates shouldn't be giving you a hard time, but if you feel there are those that can't accept you want to drink less, you could always pull the old antibiotics story, or say you're driving. This can often make the situation easier.

Avoid strong beers

Strong continental beers like Stella or Kronenbourg might seem like a great idea but they have a higher alcohol content which means you'll get more drunk and will have a worse hangover. There is sometimes a whole unit difference per pint from a lower alcohol beer.

Watch what you're drinking

Keep track of your drinks, don't line them up. Also, go for the small glass of wine, and the single shot rather than the double. Make sure you have plenty of mixers too. Try and keep shots to a minimum – they creep up and knock you out from behind.

Plan your journey home

Don't get into unlicensed minicabs, don't walk alone, don't get lifts with strangers and don't get into a car if the driver has been drinking. All sounds really sensible, doesn't it, but you'd be amazed how many people ignore this advice after lots of alcohol. Make sure you know how you're getting home before you start out.

Water before bed

A cracking final tip this one. Drink plenty of water before you go to bed and you'll thank yourself when you wake up.

Summing Up

It's a fact that children drink alcohol, and it seems certain that the problem is getting bigger all the time. Very young children are being admitted to hospital with alcohol-related troubles and the rise of binge drinking amongst teenagers and young people is alarming.

It's easy to feel invincible after you've been drinking heavily, and of course it's often quite hard to take control and keep track of what you're drinking. Everyone's having fun; you might feel like a party pooper saying no thanks. But you'll thank yourself for it in the morning and it could even save your life. So think about that.

If your child is the one drinking, communication is key. Talking is the best way to try and get through, but make sure you're on the level – talking is important but equally important, if not more so, is *listening*. Don't lecture!

Chapter Five

What Happens to Your Body?

The effects of alcohol

There are no prizes for guessing that excessive drinking is bad for you. Long term heavy drinking can lead to high blood pressure, heart disease, breast cancer, liver failure and strokes. Not much fun eh? But what actually happens to the body when you drink? Let's look at what happens on a big night out, for example.

You meet up in the pub and get the first round in

The very first drink produces a nice effect, sending the alcohol through your bloodstream and creating a pleasant feeling in your body. This is the alcohol affecting your central nervous system (CNS). Your CNS handles all your body functions including senses, speech and so on, and the early stages of intoxication during the first few hours start to interfere with this. It also affects the frontal cortex, the part of your brain that controls behaviour, so people drinking alcohol lose their inhibitions. You might speak louder, laugh a lot, talk to people more effusively, and dance with gay abandon! Further drinking affects the CNS even more, resulting in increased inability to speak clearly, stand still or walk straight.

A good few down the line

As time goes on, the effects become more severe; you sweat more, have blurred vision and your senses are dulled, including the ability to feel the sensation of pain. Alcohol is also a diuretic, which makes you urinate too much, leading to dehydration and that inevitable 'morning after' feeling.

You can't store alcohol in your body, so you have to process it via the liver. The liver can only metabolise alcohol at the rate of one unit per hour, so if you're drinking more booze than this, and not topping up the water levels in your system after going to the toilet so much, you're definitely heading for hangover city!

And yet a few more

Your reactions are slow, you are very uncoordinated and probably staggering about. You'll also get to the stage now where you might be emotional, and this can lead to aggression or perhaps being tearful. It's definitely time to go home – any more and you'll be really ill.

Crashing out

OK, so you've had a lot to drink, you're feeling very wobbly and tired, so you hit the hay. But you're not sleeping properly at all. Apart from relaxing your throat muscles, making you snore and disturbing your sleep (and those around you!), alcohol affects your sleep rhythms and patterns. You're dehydrated too, so instead of waking up and feeling refreshed, you're more likely to feel pretty ill.

Waking up

You feel tired from not sleeping properly, dehydrated which gives you headaches, and you have low levels of glucose making you feel shaky and lethargic. People crave high carbohydrate snacks the morning after, and this is because of the sugar crash.

The morning after

As the liver can only cope with a maximum of two units an hour, if you've had an absolutely massive night out the evening before, you will definitely be over the limit the next morning. Aside from this, alcohol irritates the stomach, which can lead to retching and heartburn, and affects the bowel, causing diarrhoea.

Alcohol uses up the vitamins and minerals in our system, particularly potassium, which can lead to chronic thirst, muscle cramps and lightheadedness. Being dehydrated means the kidneys have had to draw water from other organs and parts of the body, just to flush the alcohol through. This is going to make you feel headachy – achy all over actually. And the result is that your body basically produces more toxins than it can handle. You feel pretty wretched!

It's at this stage that the confirmed alcoholic or alcohol dependant will probably reach for a drink, as this method of coping – the 'hair of the dog' – is a way of staving off the results of yesterday's excess. Imagine putting your body through that trauma every day of your life.

Below is a real life case study of the physical and social damage excessive drinking can do, and how it can quickly spiral out of control.

Case study – Jane[*]

Jane was a classic binge drinker rather than a traditional alcoholic. She suffers badly from anxiety and compulsive disorders, and is terribly shy, even though she has an important job as an HR consultant. She gave up drinking at the beginning of 2008 and is attending AA meetings.

'It's weird, you know. I spend all day face to face with people, dealing with their work issues, planning events and making decisions; it's a really responsible job that I love and can handle really well.

'But when you put me in a social situation, like a night out with a group of friends, I find it really hard to deal with that. I spend hours before the time I've got to go out feeling anxious, my stomach full of butterflies, and feeling more like I just want to get under the duvet on the sofa rather than go out. Parties are the absolute worst, they fill me with complete terror. It's irrational because I know it's all my friends, but that doesn't seem to make any difference – there's no reasoning with myself over this.'

So to combat this feeling of fear, Jane often relied on alcohol to take her nerves away. Finding that a few drinks would often take the edge off her fears, she began from a very early age to use it as a prop to handle nights out.

'The trouble is, that once I start, I can't stop,' she confesses. 'It's completely out of my control in a very strange way. I have a few drinks before I leave the house so I'm already way ahead of everyone else when I get there, and you would think that I should then stop, you know, just to enjoy feeling more relaxed and start to take it easy. But it doesn't work like that. As soon as my inhibitions are removed, so is any moderation, and before I know it, I'm absolutely legless and being a complete idiot. It's like flicking a switch – there's nice normal Jane, then two or three glasses of dry white and here comes idiot drunken Jane who has a mental age of about five and is really bloody annoying.'

Jane found that her friends ran out of patience with her and she was invited out less and less.

'A few years ago, when we were all a bit younger, going out and getting drunk together was not such an unusual thing to do. We'd have a big Friday night out, start in a bar, go clubbing and stuff. But as we've got older, some of us have children, some of us have our own businesses or have got married, the whole "mad night out" thing has got less and less. But I would still drink myself stupid whatever we did. Even just going for a few drinks or dinner out with a group of mates, I would be the one who was most out of it, every time, and my mates would be putting me in cabs to send me home or whatever. If I went to someone's house for dinner, I wouldn't take just one bottle of wine, I'd take three, and then drink at least that much or more. Then I'd wake up feeling hideously embarrassed the next day.

'I'd ring up to apologise sometimes and I could feel that they were annoyed with me. It seemed like I kept ruining nights out so I think people stopped asking me along. I would hear about fun nights that others had had, but nobody would have asked me. And even though going out would make me have the fear, I would hate that I'd been left out.'

The feelings of embarrassment and remorse would often lead Jane to drink over a period of days too, something that her boyfriend struggled to deal with.

'I'd wake up feeling weird, you know, I'd know in the back of my mind something was wrong. Then the memory of the night before would come back and I'd just want to pull the duvet over my head and die. Unless I had anything particular to do I would then get up and start drinking again, just so I didn't have to think about it. Actually, whatever I had to do I would start drinking again, to be honest.

'I think I saw those days as being fun you know, a bit edgy, like it was hilarious to get legless every day of the weekend and do stupid things. But looking back, actually all it did was drive my boyfriend away and turn me into a right pain in the neck. I completely ruined loads of weekends, holidays, weekends away, even Christmases and New Year's Eves, just because I'd be drunk and spoiling it for everyone else.'

Jane made a decision to give up when she realised she was perilously close to losing everything. She found that although she was completely without restraint once she started drinking, unlike an alcoholic, she found not drinking quite easy.

'It's a weird thing but as soon as Monday morning came I was back to my normal state', she explains. 'I would be fine to get up and go to work, not drink all day, every day during the week. And have a glass of wine in the evening with dinner even. No problem, just like anyone else. But then Friday night would come around and I'd be off. Another lost weekend. Then I realised that I was going to lose my boyfriend because he was really sick of this rollercoaster, and one Sunday I woke up somewhere where I had no idea how I'd got there, my bag was missing, my clothes were torn, I had sick down my dress and to this day I still don't know what happened. I knew then I had to take control of this before it killed me or ruined my life. And everyone's life around me.'

So Jane quit, lucky enough to be one of those for whom the physical addiction is not the main issue. She has hopes that one day she might be able to relax and share a glass of wine with friends in moderation, but at the moment she is concentrating on taking control. Interestingly, those feelings of fear and anxiety when faced with social situations have diminished greatly since quitting, something she wasn't expecting.

'Because I used to dread going out, and having a couple of glasses of wine would make me feel better, I didn't think I would be able to do it without the booze, but actually it's made a big difference – not just to going out but my anxiety all round. I think the booze was making it worse, and perhaps part of the fear was knowing I was going to go out and make an idiot of myself. Anyway, I find now I can go to the bar or pub and have a nice coffee and it's completely fine. I don't stay long, not yet. It's a temptation still, but you know what? It's really loads easier than I thought. And I've been to friends' houses for dinner and drunk juice and realised that I can still have a really nice time sober. They've all been really pleased I've done this, everyone has kind of said "thank god" because they were completely fed up with it. It's been great actually. A bit weird, but overall really great.

'My outlook on life has changed a lot too. I feel a lot more positive and clear headed, plus I've lost loads of weight! I am also now going to AA meetings. I thought I wasn't an alcoholic so these meetings wouldn't apply to me, but actually it's not just about that. My boyfriend kept on about it, but I wanted to do all this myself. Then one day I thought, why not? So I spoke to someone from the AA who turned out to be completely okay so I went along. It's a real support talking to other people who know what I'm on about.'

*Names have been changed to protect identities.

How much is too much?

Current UK guidelines and drink measures from the Department of Health's Alcohol Misuse section say that men shouldn't drink more than three or four units of alcohol a day, and that for women it's even less – around two or three units a day maximum.

Don't save units for bingeing though, as this places extra pressure on your system, and do at least one alcohol free day a week – give your poor liver a chance to recover.

The quantities opposite are those quoted by the Department of Health.

One pint of strong lager
(alcohol 5% vol) = 3 units
One pint of standard strength lager
(alcohol 3 - 3.5% vol) = 2 units
One 275ml bottle of an alcopop
(alcohol 5.5% vol) = approx 1.5 units
One standard (175ml) glass of wine
(alcohol 13% vol) = 2.3 units
One pub measure of spirits
= 1 unit

What happens to your body?

You might think that once the hangover has gone, the damage is repaired. But this is not the case, and excessive drinking over a prolonged period will really start to affect your body.

Putting on weight

There are a lot of calories in alcohol, leading to weight increase. Not just that, but anyone drinking a large amount will often have poor eating habits – late night forays to the kebab shop or curry house, for example. You might also eat more than is necessary at home of the wrong kind of food.

Your skin

Being dehydrated all the time is going to have an effect on your skin – it will become dry and dull. Alcohol also dilates your capillaries, the tiny veins just under the surface of your skin, which can break, leading to unsightly redness and broken veins on the face. Very attractive!

'Being dehydrated all the time is going to have an effect on your skin – it will become dry and dull. Alcohol also dilates your capillaries, the tiny veins just under the surface of your skin, which can break, leading to unsightly redness and broken veins on the face. Very attractive!'

The eyes have it

Not only does alcohol affect the capillaries in your face, but it also damages the blood vessels in your eyes. Bloodshot eyes are a common side effect of drinking too much.

Smelling bad

You know that morning after smell? Your poor liver struggles to process all the alcohol and your body tries to help out by excreting it through sweat, urine and of course, your breath.

Battered body

Serious boozers are accident prone and often violent. Cuts, bruises, broken bones and scars are all part of the pattern.

Long term

I think anyone reading this book is going to know by now that excessive drinking over a long period of time is bad for you. If you know you have a drink problem, read this carefully. It's not just about having hangovers – the damage can be far worse, and can accelerate or cause any of the following conditions:

- Cirrhosis of the liver or liver cancer.
- Breast cancer.
- Heart muscle damage (cardiomyopathy).
- High blood pressure.
- Obesity.
- Infertility.
- Cerebral haemorrhage (stroke).
- Coronary heart disease.
- Blood pressure, stress, diabetes, liver disease.

'Alcohol uses up the vitamins and minerals in your system, particularly potassium, which can lead to chronic thirst, muscle cramps and light-headedness.'

- Sexual difficulties, including impotence.

- Pancreatitis.

- Stomach problems such as ulcers.

- Potentially fatal alcohol poisoning.

It's not just about the physical effects though. Drinking a lot of alcohol over a length of time will also affect your mental state, causing the following problems:

- Depression.

- Suicidal feelings.

- Personality deterioration.

- Poor concentration.

- Sexual performance problems.

- Dementia and mental impairments.

- Hallucination.

- Memory loss.

- Mood changes.

What to do in an emergency

Drinking a large amount at one time can lead to unconsciousness, coma, and even death. It's one of the least recognised emergencies and is often dealt with inefficiently if those around the victim are also drunk.

If you are with someone you know has been drinking heavily, and the symptoms include vomiting, sweating, laboured or shallow breathing or unconsciousness, you need to act.

Firstly, place the victim in the recovery position. If you don't know what this is, it basically means lying the person on their side. Allowing them to lie on their back can mean vomit could choke them. Then ring for help, immediately. Call for an ambulance and stay with the person. Make sure you can hear them breathing and check their pulse. If the victim vomits, try to ensure that the airways remain clear so they don't suffocate on it. Stay calm and wait for help.

'Long term heavy drinking can lead to high blood pressure, heart disease, breast cancer, liver failure and strokes.'

Summing Up

Alcohol is really bad for you in large doses, and even worse over a long period of time. Learning to cope with an emergency could help save someone's life, but it's also important, whether you're an alcoholic or living with someone with a drink problem, to know what alcohol does to your body.

Long term, the prognosis isn't good. Heart disease, cancer, liver disease and all those real bad guys are all there for the alcohol abuser. The good news is that stopping can really make a difference and, cleverly, the liver has a way of mending and regenerating itself.

Chapter Six

Foetal Alcohol Syndrome

The first case of Foetal Alcohol Syndrome (FAS) was diagnosed in the late 70s and was based on WHO estimates. However, it's now thought that there could be as many as 450,000 people living in Britain with the condition.

The odd glass of wine during pregnancy isn't usually going to have a drastic effect, but according to Dr Raja Mukherjee, a psychiatrist specialising in FAS, even moderate amounts can have an effect. The only completely safe amount is none at all.

The damage

Children born with FAS are highly likely to be underweight and premature. Birth defects are common, as are physical abnormalities such as skeletal weakness or neurological damage.

How bad the damage is will depend on how heavy the intake is, generally. Women who drink heavily and repeatedly throughout their pregnancy are risking damaging their babies and the effects will last a lifetime.

As children with FAS grow up, they can have trouble engaging with their peers and can feel isolated. Their mental age will be affected and they will have trouble developing emotionally. They stand a high chance of being bullied or ostracised.

Memory can be affected too, with the sufferer having problems retaining information or losing short term memory. Bones are smaller and weaker.

Overall, the effects can be quite devastating, with the general impression being of a person who is not drastically unwell, but just not functioning properly on most or many levels. It makes life hard.

With so many children being increasingly diagnosed with Attention Deficit Disorder, Susan Fleisher of the National Association on Foetal Alcohol Syndrome has raised a possibility that FAS could be the reason for the rise. 'We are seeing children at nursery with attention deficit disorder who could be the products of mothers who had a binge drink three years earlier, before they knew they were pregnant,' she explains. She also believes that it could be binge drinking during pregancy that has lead to the rise in crime amongst older children, with the rise of binge drinking among young women having a direct effect on the children they are bearing. It's an interesting theory that definitely gives pause for thought.

Alcohol and the foetus

'Experts believe that alcohol can be more dangerous than cocaine or heroin to an unborn child.'

When a pregnant mother drinks alcohol, the molecules are so small that they easily pass through the placenta where they kill off nerve endings and the connections between the brain cells, leading to permanent damage.

In severe cases, symptoms include underweight babies; slow growth rate; deformed ears; small eyes; slow development of the optic nerve and short-sightedness; skeletal defects; heart damage; a small head; a thin upper lip and small teeth and mental retardation.

In less severe cases, babies can also show other signs of Foetal Alcohol Spectrum Disorder such as immature behaviour; hyperactivity; having a lower IQ, poor short-term memory; problems with abstract concepts; poor coordination and difficulty with social and emotional relationships.

A lot depends on physical and genetic makeup. Some babies will cope with their mothers consuming alcohol much better than others. This is also affected by the mother's general health and well-being, and at what stage of the pregnancy the alcohol consumption is, with the early stages being where the mother is most vulnerable.

But whenever drinking takes place, it can have a detrimental effect. During the early stages for example, it can lead to physical deformities as this is when the face and skeleton are forming. But during later stages, the nervous system can be affected, leading to low IQ or brain damage.

Summing Up

When pregnant, it's easy to feel left out of fun and frolics, and it may be tempting to drink along with your friends or keep up with old drinking habits. It might be the case too that you are an alcoholic who will find giving up just as hard as it would be normally, pregnant or not. Perhaps your partner has an alcohol abuse problem and you're worried about your unborn child.

Getting help for a drink problem is always going to be a good idea, but it's even more important when pregnant. It's not just your life and health that is under threat, but you could cause permanent and debilitating damage to the person you are carrying. People with FAS have long term problems and can be completely dysfunctional, leading to unhappy and difficult lives. Imagine living with that on your conscience.

Seek medical help – whether it's you with the problem or your partner. Your GP is a good place to start. It's vital that you take care of yourself during pregnancy, and even if you lapse back afterwards, at least you can feel more positive that you have given the baby a better head start. It's all about individual steps and this would be a very, very good step to take.

Chapter Seven

Dealing with the Reality

Is it me?

Living with somebody who is alcohol dependent or being an alcohol dependant yourself is no picnic. It's particularly hard for children where one of their parents is the one with the problem – they can see their friends having normal, happy lives, but their own home will be chaotic, disordered, often filled with arguments and usually a stressful place to be. It's very difficult for them to come to terms with this when it's impossible to see a good reason for all the turmoil.

Partners and children often look to themselves and their own behaviour to try to identify a source for it all, wondering perhaps if they behaved differently, would the problem go away. The 'why me?' question rings in their heads; they cannot fathom why it is happening. Surely the drinker can see the damage they're doing?

It's hard to realise when this happens that it's not your fault and nothing you have done has caused this. It's also good to be aware that, although you can be around to support an alcoholic's decision to change, you will never be the one to activate that decision. It absolutely has to come from the addict.

For anyone who has come to terms with the fact that they have an addiction of this type, it's also equally hard to understand why it has happened to them too. 'Why me?' is just as potent a question for them, and they will struggle to understand what makes them like this.

'Partners and children often look to themselves and their own behaviour to try to identify a source for the addiction, wondering perhaps if they behaved differently, would the problem go away.'

'In order to preserve some kind of semblance of respectability, the family of an alcoholic will often seek to try and cover up the problem too, unfortunately aiding and abetting the addiction in the process. They don't want all and sundry to see that there is a problem and so lies are told, excuses are made and messes cleared up or explained away.'

Social embarrassment

Social drinking is seen as a shared and fun thing to do. A glass of wine at dinner, champagne at a wedding, a few too many at a party – all of these things are acceptable social variables, but dealing with continuous excessive drinking is most definitely not okay. The behaviour that goes with it can be embarrassing for both the drinker and those around them, leading to remorse on the part of the perpetrator and mortification for everyone else. (Remember Jane's story.)

Public appearances can be a minefield, with the alcoholic pretty much hell bent on simply drinking as much as they can to get through it, or possibly even turning up drunk. Equally though, friends and neighbours at home will find the whole thing a bit much to deal with, and social invitations to parties and dinners will certainly be in short supply. After all, who wants someone as volatile as the alcoholic at the dinner table? You have no idea what they're going to say or do next.

In order to preserve some kind of semblance of respectability, the family of an alcoholic will often seek to try and cover up the problem too, unfortunately aiding and abetting the addiction in the process. They don't want all and sundry to see that there is a problem and so lies are told, excuses are made and messes cleared up or explained away.

However, no matter how awful their behaviour might have been, and how embarrassing it has been for all concerned, one of the major factors the alcoholic faces when confronting their problem is the stigma of being labelled as someone with a 'drink problem'. Although the feelings associated with alcohol dependence can include a sense of isolation or shame, for them, owning up to it and going public can be equally difficult.

Owning up to it

It is very often the case that the last person to admit there is a problem is the alcoholic. And, I'm sorry to say, this sometimes never happens at all. Some alcohol dependants will go on living with the addiction and never come to terms with it, or ever end up dealing with it.

According to Prochaska and DiClemente, the path that the recovering alcoholic will usually tread is broken down into five recognisable stages; Pre-contemplation, Contemplation, Preparation, Action and Maintenance. If you live with an alcoholic, this will help you identify and understand the stages.

Pre-contemplation

This is the stage where denial is still strong. The alcoholic will reject any suggestion that there is a problem, usually being angry and defensive about it. They will throw out any proposal of treatment and seek out drinking buddies or situations that help them maintain or conceal a high intake of alcohol. They will try to refute any kind of suggestion that they need help and their life will be chaotic.

Contemplation

This often happens once things have got really bad, or there has been a crisis of some sort, and the drinker is faced with the undeniable fact that they have a problem. This is often a real sock in the jaw, with the alcohol dependant slowly coming to the realisation that things have to change, and change for good. It's also a key time for depression and anxiety to kick in, as there will be an overwhelming sense of the enormity of what's happened and happening. It's really hard for them to face up to this.

Preparation

At preparation stage, the alcoholic will start to look at the ways to move forward. It's a positive stage, but depending on the severity, it can be really daunting. Severe alcoholism is going to cause intense physical reaction and, for all, some level of detox is needed. Some will need in-patient care and medication for the withdrawal. Most will need addiction counselling and support, and often other forms of therapy such as marital or family counselling will be needed to help repair any damage done to loved ones around.

'One of the major factors the alcoholic faces when confronting their problem is the stigma of being labelled as someone with a "drink problem". Although the feelings associated with alcohol dependence can include a sense of isolation or shame, going public can be equally difficult.'

Action

Now the alcoholic has to put all this into action. Friends and family are paramount to support and help this stage, and it's not unusual for action to be short-lived or followed soon after by relapse. Basically, it could take a few goes to get it right and make it stick.

Maintenance

This final, ongoing stage is vital. In order to stay on the right path, the recovered alcoholic needs to stay alert to potential areas of temptation, such as going out with old drinking partners, having booze around the house, stressful situations that would normally have them reaching for the bottle and so on. Support groups such as Alcoholics Anonymous can be invaluable for this lengthy, sometimes infinite stage, as the understanding and empathy of those in the same boat can give a much needed prop.

Summing Up

We will look in more detail at the support groups available in chapter 10, and widely recognised as approved or respected avenues of support are listed at the back of this book. But take heart. Once an alcoholic has made a decision to get help and has put this into action, there is a good chance things will work out okay.

Facing up to friends, family and colleagues is never going to be easy, but often the alcoholic will find relief from the fact that the problem is finally being addressed and they are being supported by people who have been desperately worried about them. Yes, that person is always going to wear the 'ex-drinker' label, but that is a million times better than living with the hell of addiction.

If it's you who has come to this realisation, you can give yourself a massive pat on the back; you're about to make a fantastic change. Try to remain positive, but be realistic and take one day at a time.

The path to recovery is never easy, and relapses often happen. But making that decision to change is the hardest part. Anyone who has reached that decision can feel very proud of themselves straightaway.

Chapter Eight

Help for Children

Children of alcoholics

This might seem like stating the obvious, but a 2006 report by the UK addiction specialists, Priority Healthcare, revealed that children who have grown up with alcoholic parents bear fundamental emotional and behavioural scars.

Anyone who has lived with an alcoholic mother or father will know what a rollercoaster home life can become. Children can find themselves blamed for the problem as the alcoholic seeks to point the finger at others; they live with arguments, chaos, confusion and shame. It's also a tragic fact that alcohol contributes heavily to the occurrence of abuse, both sexual and physical.

The Priory consulted its own doctors and therapists to compile the report, but also took into account existing figures on crime, abuse and alcoholism. According to the study, 55% of domestic violence happened in alcoholic homes and 90% of child abuse cases involved alcohol abuse. It also found that girls were up to four times more likely to suffer sexual abuse in an alcoholic home.

Research into previous studies undertaken as part of the Priory report discovered that 70% of those children with alcohol abuse in their homes went on to develop compulsive behaviour themselves, whether it might be addictions to alcohol, drugs, gambling, sex or even food – and about half of them ended up marrying or living with alcoholics or alcohol abusers when they grew up.

Unsurprisingly, children of alcoholics were found to be four times more likely to become alcoholics themselves, partly perhaps due to genetics but also because of learnt behaviour – although of course this is not a foregone conclusion and should never be seen as such.

The report said children react in one of three ways. They may become quiet or withdrawn, they may live in denial, or may use their background to their advantage by becoming stronger. However, whatever outward composure they might have is purely that – outward – and the report states: 'Their feelings about themselves are the opposite of the serene image they present – they generally feel insecure, inadequate, dull, unsuccessful, vulnerable and anxious.' The report also discovered that they found it difficult to develop strong personal relationships.

What is perhaps most staggering about the study is that the general average for people with this destructive illness is estimated at around 1 in 20. So if you are one of those children who has a parent suffering from this condition, please don't feel alone. It's much more common than you think and there is a lot of help out there.

> 'Living with an alcoholic is tough - but you are definitely not alone. Studies conducted by the National Association for Children of Alcoholics show that there are close to a million people under the age of 18 in the UK living with parents who have an alcohol problem.'

Is your parent an alcoholic?

Alcoholism is a family disease. It's something you'll hear a lot in circles that know about this kind of thing, and what it means is just that. If there is someone with an alcohol problem in your family, it affects every single member. When things are good, everyone is happy, when alcohol rears its head, the whole household suffers.

60

If you live with this, you will understand that completely. Coming home becomes a journey of fear – what is waiting for you when you get back? Night times are frightening, listening in bed for the sounds of arguments or violence. Or worse, fearing for your own safety from attack or abuse. Or you might simply feel saddened watching someone you love wasting their life, focused on alcohol and seemingly not much else. You could also find yourself assuming responsibility in the house, as nobody else seems to bother. If you don't get yourself some dinner and wash your school uniform, who will?

You probably won't want to have your mates round for fear of embarrassment and there's every chance that you're getting the blame for all this, that it's your fault mum or dad drink. It's not much fun, is it?

You're not alone

Living with an alcoholic is tough - but you are definitely not alone. Studies conducted by the National Association for Children of Alcoholics have shown that there are close to a million people under the age of 18 in the UK living with parents who have an alcohol problem.

- You might feel like hiding the problem from the world or that it's your fault, but you mustn't.

- Try not to feel embarrassed or ashamed about the person who is an alcoholic – alcoholism is a disease and it's absolutely not your fault.

- They need help, but do be aware you can't change things or make them stop drinking – that decision has to come from them.

Talk to someone

One of the things children or teenagers in this situation often do is to keep it all to themselves. They don't talk to other people about their situation, preferring to keep a low profile. But one of the strongest pieces of advice I could give you is to talk to someone.

Apart from the relief of letting it all out, you might find that the person you talk to can help you. It could be a teacher you trust at school or college, a friend's mum or dad, a family friend or another relative. Having their support and

'Find someone to talk to. Apart from the relief of letting it all out, you might find that the person you talk to can help you, offer support and maybe a place to run to when things are bad.'

understanding will give you strength, and they may be able to offer practical help as well, such as someone to come to when times are bad – a bolt-hole when you need some peace and quiet, or safety.

Another way to help you deal with what's going on at home is to get involved with some fun stuff outside home, and away from school too. Get out more, try to enjoy life and immerse yourself in doing things that will make you feel better about yourself and cheer you up. It's important to develop your own potential, whatever anyone else says at home. Don't let it hold you back.

Tips for an easier life

To make life easier at home, try to avoid arguments when your parents have been drinking and don't attempt to try and stop the drinking, either by hiding drink or pouring it away. It won't work, honestly. It's just going to cause further strife.

And finally, very importantly, recognise that it's okay to feel both love and hate for the person with the alcohol problem. It's completely normal for anyone in this situation, so don't beat yourself up about it – you're going to be upset and angry a lot of the time. But there are ways to detach yourself from the drinking part, and still love that person for who they are, aside from the drinking. Support groups can help you understand and accept that too, which in turn will make it easier to cope at home.

Are you worried about someone else's children?

It could be that you know a family with an alcohol problem, and if there are children or teenagers involved, you want to try and help in some way.

How you proceed with this will depend very much on who you are and who you are worried about. If you're a teacher, a friend of the family or a relative, and the child or children are old enough to relate to you directly, it might be that you can have a chat with them. Ask them gently about any problems and let them know you are there. Be prepared for initial rejection though – it's very normal for children in this situation to be in denial or embarrassed. In time they may come around and, when that happens, it's important for them to know that you are available to help them, in whatever way you can.

But what if you're not close to the family, or if the children involved are infants? You could be seriously worried about physical or sexual abuse going on in the home and really want to help, but don't know how to.

I can't give you advice on this, but there are definitely groups that you can talk to about how to deal with this. A really good place to start would be the National Association for Children of Alcoholics. Visit www.nacoa.org.uk or call freephone 0800 358 3456.

Don't delay though, and be strong about it. If there are children in real danger, the appropriate authorities will need to be contacted as soon as possible – regardless of how close your relationship might be with the family. You might feel like you're betraying someone, but it's absolutely vital that children are protected from abuse, whoever the perpetrator is. Imagine if you did nothing and the worst happened.

Children's support options

As the child of an alcoholic, you might feel pretty powerless. It's true to say that you can't make your parent or carer stop drinking – that has to come from them. But there are ways to help cope with the chaos and unhappiness.

We've already talked about family, friends or teachers who could be the shoulder you need, but there are other options too.

There are support groups set up specifically for children and teenagers of alcoholics, such as Alateen, which is part of Al-Anon. This helps the younger members of families with alcohol problems and friends of alcoholics.

As I've already mentioned, there's also the National Association for Children of Alcoholics (www.nacoa.org.uk) which has a freephone helpline 0800 358 3456.

Please also know that nearly a quarter of the calls the NACOA gets are from seven-year-olds, so don't think this freephone number is only for older children. If you need to talk, you can just pick up the phone.

In the help list at the back of the book there are loads of useful numbers and websites, so check these out – there are people who can help you.

Summing Up

There is no doubt that being the child of an alcoholic parent – or in some cases both parents – is pretty tough and, for some, life is unbearable. Eventually of course you will be old enough to leave it all behind, but there are ways to cope whilst you have no choice but to remain.

Keep a level head, remember it's absolutely not your fault, and try to find interests outside the home that you can enjoy. Things change and you may find that your mum or dad makes a change for the better, or perhaps it's simply the time when you can move out that you will be looking forward to, but above all, find someone you can talk to.

If you're the parent, you will probably know already that alcohol abuse will damage your children and if you're reading this, you're highly likely to have made a decision to change all that. But if it's someone else's children you're worried about as you read this, don't delay in seeking advice. You could make a real difference to someone's life.

Chapter Nine

Sorting it Out

Making the decision

Deciding to give up alcohol is the first and biggest leap along the road to recovery. It's the hardest thing the alcoholic will ever do, making that choice, and should be recognised as such. Making the decision to quit the booze is not something anyone else can do for a person who is alcohol dependent; the only person who can make that decision is them. Having said that, once that choice has been made, it will inevitably involve all those around that person too. So if it's you giving up, be aware of that.

Though making the decision is the hardest part, it's not like the rest of the journey is going to be a walk in the park. Once the decision has been made, the next step is to form some kind of plan; work out whether you'll need help with the physical effects of withdrawal; plan how your counselling or support strategy will work and put in place incentives and deterrents to help avoid falling off the wagon as time progresses.

I want to give up

Cold turkey

Going cold turkey alone is hard, and for someone who is heavily dependent it's potentially quite dangerous because of the withdrawal symptoms. So start to look into options for medical support and ensure aftercare is in place once the severe withdrawal symptoms have passed. Years of drinking will have taken their toll on your body and it will be a while before you are fully well.

'Once the decision has been made, the next step is to form some kind of plan; work out whether you'll need help with the physical effects of withdrawal; plan how your counselling or support strategy will work and put in place incentives and deterrents to help avoid falling off the wagon as time progresses.'

If you think you can safely come off drinking at home, start to make some plans for that. Clear the house of alcohol so you won't be tempted, and maybe leave your cash or cards with someone else to make it really hard to buy alcohol. Take time off work for this – if you're employed, you're not going to be at your best for a few days. Alcohol also has a high sugar content and you'll feel the dip in the supply of glucose, so stock up on soft drinks and fruit juices to replace that sugar content. This will help with the shakes and so on.

Cutting back

It doesn't have to be such a severe method as this sudden stopping though, and many have found it easier to cut down before giving up. This reduces the level of physical reliance on alcohol, but needs careful monitoring or managing as it's easy for the quantity to start to creep up again.

The best way to use this method is to schedule a clear strategy and timeline, setting goals for how much to reduce by for certain dates and sticking to it. Put a time limit on the period of reduction too, otherwise you can fall into the trap of starting to think you're okay drinking in moderation. It'll rise again, believe me, and you'll be back to square one. Remember it's only a temporary state and make sure you stick to your goals. Don't ever forget your ultimate goal is to give up completely.

Telling friends and family

There's a good chance that you might feel 'going public' is going to leave you open to judgement by friends and family. You might also feel perhaps that it's embarrassing to have to admit to a drink problem. But in many or even most cases you will find that actually everyone knows what's going on already and are just very glad to see you finally dealing with it.

Being under the influence of alcohol on a regular and frequent basis will have clouded your judgement to a greater or lesser degree, but it's not uncommon for alcohol abusers to be unaware of the impact that they are having on those around them. Of course you will have some understanding of the pressure it's put your immediate family under, but you may be surprised to see how far-reaching the effects of your behaviour will have been.

Explain to your friends and family what you are doing and ask for their help. Having their support at this time is really constructive and far easier than going it alone.

What to expect

The first thing to understand is that quitting drinking is going to cause some withdrawal symptoms. Anyone who is alcohol dependent will experience some unpleasantness – those with milder addictions will have less severe symptoms of course, but for heavy or very long term alcohol abuse, going cold turkey can be pretty rough. Those symptoms can include the following:

Withdrawal symptoms

Mild to moderate symptoms:

- Being jumpy, shaky, anxious.
- Headaches, sweating, having palpitations.
- Nausea or vomiting.
- Being irritable or overemotional.
- Depression.
- Tiredness and/or insomnia.
- Difficulty with focusing or thinking clearly.
- Bad dreams.
- Loss of appetite.

Severe symptoms:

- Confused, agitated mental state.
- Hallucinations (visual) also known as delirium tremens.
- Fever.
- Ranting and violence.
- Convulsions.

'Being under the influence of alcohol on a regular and frequent basis will have clouded your judgement to a greater or lesser degree, but it's not uncommon for an alcohol abuser to be unaware of the impact that he or she is having on those around them.'

If you're a heavy user, you're going to need medical help, so make sure you put that in place before starting – you're far better off somewhere where there are qualified medics to help you and it could be dangerous to do this at home.

Aside from the physical effects of withdrawal, there is the psychological issue too. The little voice that tells you to give up giving up, that feeling like this is far worse than having a drink, so why bother? It's a very persuasive voice and many alcoholics who try to give up alone find they are not strong enough to resist it.

Don't be disheartened. If it takes several goes to kick it, so what? Better to kick it than not, so don't give up. Above all, remember that it does get easier; the withdrawal symptoms are at their worst for a maximum of one week, often less, and after that things will start to get better. What's one week out of your life?

Treatment

Very severe cases

The number of people who need hospitalisation for withdrawal from alcohol is very small. If you are in that small minority, you will pretty much need to put yourself in the hands of the experts and buckle up for the ride. There's no point in fudging this, it's going to be tough. But as I've said before, it only lasts a short while and you'll be in good hands.

In the hospital or treatment centre you can expect to be kept in for some days. You will have heart, blood pressure, breathing etc monitored, and, if needed, medication such as tranquillisers. You'll also be given fluids and electrolytes to replace lost minerals. Once the worst is over and you're physically stronger, you'll be able to go home, where you'll start the ongoing process of rehabilitation. It's not just about giving up drinking, it's about rediscovering the world outside the bottle again, and this in itself can be hard. It's really about learning to live all over again.

Rehab will normally involve support groups, counselling or therapy (or both) and possibly medication. The more you accept the support available, the more chance you have of staying dry. Those that go it alone are far more likely to fall off the wagon.

'Anyone who is alcohol dependent will experience some unpleasantness – those with milder addictions will have less severe symptoms of course, but for heavy or very long term alcohol abuse, going cold turkey can be pretty rough.'

Need2Know

Giving up at home

Mostly people are fine to quit at home, with the biggest danger coming from the psychological temptation to start drinking again. However, it's always good practice to seek medical advice before giving up, and having someone keeping an eye on you will help strengthen your resolve too. Your doctor will be able to advise you on ways to avoid some of the physical effects such as shaking or restlessness and may prescribe beta blockers or sleeping tablets to help, but this will depend on each patient.

If you're doing the home thing, you'll find the first three days will probably be the worst. You might be anxious, irritable and restless, and you'll probably experience flu-like symptoms. You'll also find sleep elusive. Alcohol affects natural sleeping patterns, and when you stop you will probably find you are very wakeful, being only able to sleep for a few hours at a time.

Take to the sofa, watch telly and sleep when you can. Eventually your natural rhythms will reassert themselves and you'll be able to get a good night's sleep.

Summing Up

It's never going to be a breeze giving up. Even mild symptoms like cravings or anxiety are little fun, and the severe cases are going to be very uncomfortable.

The best way to tackle all this is to be prepared. Cutting down before quitting can help; take time off work if you need it; make sure you have friends and family about and get some counselling or therapy.

Be positive too. When you have dark days – and you will – remember the reasons for quitting. Perhaps you can even keep a list to remind yourself.

If you're in the supporting role whilst someone else is giving up, prepare yourself too. It's not going to be pretty! Remember not to take any abuse that is hurled at you personally and be aware that the physical symptoms of withdrawal can be scary. It will all be well worth it though.

Chapter Ten

The Recovery Options

Rehabilitation and residential treatment

Rehab has rather been popularised by troubled celebrities, and sometimes a huge part of giving up drinking can be just having the chance to get away from it all, in privacy. Space and time to recover, with specialists on hand 24 hours a day can feel really safe, and be a positive way to address the issues. But what can really make a difference is breaking patterns. Well-worn or familiar drinking routines at home will remind you daily of the thing you're giving up, and rehab can give you time to break the habits and rediscover the old you, the sober you.

Residential rehab units have fully trained members of staff such as nurses, therapists, counsellors and security, all of whom specialise in addiction management, so you'll know that rather than getting general medical support, you're being offered a specialised form of treatment.

For those around a recovering alcoholic, knowing that the person is being taken care of in a residential treatment centre can give great peace of mind. It can also offer a welcome break if there has been ongoing and relentless discord in the home, giving everyone a chance to draw a deep breath and let go of all the pain for a bit.

Successful rehabilitation will depend largely on how much commitment and input the patient brings to it, although you can of course accept that this will go for the whole 'giving up' process; it's never going to be like falling off a log – there is hard work involved. But rehab will offer alcoholics a chance to face life without alcohol, and show people how they can live again without their own particular brand of poison.

'For those around a recovering alcoholic, knowing that the person is being taken care of in a residential treatment centre can give great peace of mind. It can also offer a welcome break.'

The rehab centres will offer structured support with counselling and therapy, not just dealing with breaking the addiction itself, but helping sufferers accept the change that life will undergo, and offering motivational support and ongoing treatment to help prevent relapsing. Psychosocial skills support might also be available, as just learning to communicate with and relate to people all over again after a long period of drinking can be a challenge in itself.

Private rehabilitation and residential treatment centres are pretty pricey, but well worth it if you can afford them. There are also options available on the NHS or through social services for people with severe alcoholism and related conditions. Very often you will find a criminal sentence will involve some kind of mandatory rehab term – a very common occurrence in the case of alcohol-related crime. Many residential centres will have an option where you may be able to get some or part of the treatment funded by the state, but it will be means tested. Basically if you can afford to go, you have to pay.

Often a rehab centre will specialise in one or two particular types of addiction – alcohol is the most common and most centres will offer treatment for alcohol dependency cases.

How rehab works

Patients must arrive sober, clean and free from alcohol. The centre will not accept them rolling up after 'one last drink'! There is likely to be a search to make sure there are no hidden bottles, and the patient will have to sign a contract committing them to not drinking at all during their stay.

The staff at the rehab centre will be able to prescribe medication to help with any intense withdrawal symptoms and to assist with detoxing the system. This is likely to be short term though and the next stage is to start counselling and therapy to identify underlying issues and hopefully the cause of the dependency.

The centre will often try to involve the family of a recovering alcoholic, so that they understand the underlying principles of recovery and maintenance. But this will only be once the patient is clean and has gone through the period of detox and withdrawal.

'Being single minded and committed is the biggest requirement for quitting, so although residential rehab seems like a softer option, the bottom line is that without that commitment, it doesn't matter where you are.'

Non-residential recovery

Giving up without the 'luxury' of residential rehab is, of course, entirely possible, and is the way that most people tackle the problem. All of the options – therapy, medication, etc – are available in the outside world too! Being single minded and committed is the biggest requirement for quitting, so although residential rehab seems like a softer option, the bottom line is that without that commitment, it doesn't matter where you are.

Alcoholics Anonymous and the 12 Steps

The 12 Step method was popularised by Alcoholics Anonymous (AA) but is now used widely throughout most support groups including Al-Anon, which is for the family members and loved ones of alcoholics, and Narcotics Anonymous, which is for drug addicts. Alateen also offers the same thing for teenagers and older children with alcoholic parents. The programme has proved to be widely successful, with many of these groups basing themselves around the 12 Step method adapted to the support role, rather than being aimed at the sufferer.

The 12 Steps, as designated by the AA:

1. We admitted we were powerless over alcohol - that our lives had become unmanageable.

2. Came to believe that a Power greater than ourselves could restore us to sanity.

3. Made a decision to turn our will and our lives over to the care of God as we understood Him.

4. Made a searching and fearless moral inventory of ourselves.

5. Admitted to God, to ourselves and to another human being the exact nature of our wrongs.

6. Were entirely ready to have God remove all these defects of character.

7. Humbly asked Him to remove our shortcomings.

'The AA started in around 1935 with just a few members, and now has over 2 million members worldwide.'

8. Made a list of all persons we had harmed, and became willing to make amends to them all.

9. Made direct amends to such people wherever possible, except when to do so would injure them or others.

10. Continued to take personal inventory and when we were wrong promptly admitted it.

11. Sought through prayer and meditation to improve our conscious contact with God as we understood Him, praying only for knowledge of His will for us and the power to carry that out.

12. Having had a spiritual awakening as the result of these steps, we tried to carry this message to alcoholics and to practice these principles in all our affairs.

© Copyright Alcoholics Anonymous. Visit www.alcoholics-anonymous.org for more information on the 12 Step method and how to join AA.

As you can see, a lot of this is based very firmly in seeking spiritual guidance, and many can be put off by the overt religious overtones of the 12 Steps. AA are at great pains to point out that nobody is forced to follow these guidelines if they don't want to and will still be welcomed with open arms.

It may be that you are prepared and happy to accept these steps. But if not, the best way to approach this might be to look at the underlying meaning in each step. It's pretty easy to remove the religious structure from most of the points and still be able to tackle what's covered – such as admitting the problem (Step 1), making an inventory of yourself (Step 4) or making amends (Steps 8 – 10)

12 Steps won't be for everyone, but the success of AA's track record is undeniable. It's very much about going on a journey of recovery and they do use words like 'fellowship' and 'reaching', which can be a bit cringey! However, the AA asks that you keep an open mind and aim to interpret the steps as best you can.

They also have a total abstinence policy, pointing out that alcoholism is a disease and there is no cure. The only way to control it and stop it in its tracks is by giving up completely. There's no compromise.

Not all non-residential support is through the AA though, and you may find a different group that suits you better. Talk to your GP about this as they may be able to suggest some alternatives in your area.

Support for family and friends

Support is out there for those around the alcoholic too. Very often family and friends will be left feeling angry, worried, devastated or resentful. Living with an alcohol abuser can be very difficult and although you might be happy to see that person taking control and facing up to it, you will find all kinds of emotions welling up from years of unhappiness or strife in the home.

You are not expected to just be able to let go of that. A big part of the alcoholic's rehabilitation will often be therapy. Family therapy is highly recommended, as you can have a chance to go through this together.

But something that's purely for yourself, to help you heal, will be important too. There are support groups specifically for those around the alcoholic such as Al-Anon, or Alateen for younger members, which are both part of Alcoholics Anonymous. But check around, you might find something that suits you better.

It could well be worth talking this over with your GP too, and asking for counselling or therapy on your own behalf. Do not underestimate how damaging long term alcohol abuse can be on those around the person drinking, and make sure you look after yourself. Remember that the alcoholic is going to need ongoing support too and you will need to be strong to cope. You're not superhuman and you must attend to your own needs as well – to nurture yourself.

Types of therapy

All the various recommended forms of therapy are available within residential rehab centres, but if you're not using such a centre, they can still be accessed – for example, through your doctor or with Alcoholics Anonymous.

One to one counselling

This is exactly what it sounds like; simply a case of having a sympathetic ear as you talk over problems. Counselling differs from therapy in as much as it's more of a listening situation, with prompting, rather than deeper analysis or probing of the problem. Sometimes it's just enough to get things off your chest.

Group counselling

This is where a group will sit together and share feelings or experiences. Some people find this method helpful, knowing that there are others with similar problems. But equally, there are others who find the public aspect of sharing very hard.

Cognitive behavioural therapy

The word 'cognitive' relates to conscious intellectual activity. This therapy prods patients to remember, understand and resolve things, and to do it for themselves. It can often be a rollercoaster of a process, going through some painful memories or background, but essentially it gets to the root of the problem.

Psychosocial therapy

Being drunk a lot means you're not acting normally, and suddenly you will find yourself sober and maybe unable to relate to people the way you used to. Psychosocial therapy will help a patient to redevelop those interpersonal skills needed to communicate with the outside world again.

Family/marriage therapy

It goes without saying that the alcohol dependant is usually not the only one who has been damaged by the addiction, and family or relationship counselling can be a huge part of recovery. Helping those around to understand it better, and giving everyone a chance to go through the issues raised by the problem, can help to repair damage to family members too.

Summing Up

Basically the methods of rehabilitation are the same across the board, whether you can afford or qualify for residential care or not. Detox, followed by counselling and therapy, will be the cornerstones for the recovery period, with ongoing counselling recommended to stay focused.

Remember though, it's not just the alcoholic that is in need of help and support. Anyone affected by this family illness is going to need a boost too, and rehab will apply to everybody involved, without exception.

Chapter Eleven
The Future

No going back

Hopefully, once the alcoholic has passed the stage of detox and craving and is well on the way to rehabilitation, they will feel much better about themselves and recovery will start to run a bit more smoothly. They should do – it's a real achievement and they should be very pleased to have made such a positive move. And those around them will certainly find life is easier. Whatever the level of addiction or whatever the behavioural issues have been, having that person sober is always going to be better than the alternative.

For each individual case, quitting drinking is going to raise different issues and unlock different experiences and emotions. Some will just be relieved and thankful to have got it sorted out, some angry with themselves or terrified of going back, others proud to have conquered the beast… but one thing they are all aware of and should agree on is that there is no going back.

If you're reading this as an alcoholic, remember that once you've kicked the habit, then that's it – you need to accept that you cannot drink again. Alcohol is not something you can take lightly – there is no 'odd drink' for the truly addicted. It's much easier to start again than not, and resisting temptation is hard. But, having made that positive step forward, taking even one drink is potentially disastrous.

Buddies

A buddy is a voluntary mentor who can help and support a recovering addict through rehab. They will be the person a recovering alcoholic can ring to talk about their experiences if they feel tempted, or if they fall off the wagon. A buddy will be someone who has kicked the same habit and stuck to it, so they truly know the score.

If you are the one needing help, this support will be invaluable. It's particularly good for those without close family to support them, as an addition to an already pressurised family unit, or perhaps for those who feel put off by groups. In darker hours or when you need to let off steam, a buddy can make a real difference.

Non-judgmental and a walking testimony to the fact that the habit can be licked, and stay licked, an addict in recovery can often really connect with a buddy, recognising that the buddy can completely understand what they're going through. With the best will in the world, family and friends can be sympathetic, but have no real notion of your experience and ongoing battle.

If you are, say, the spouse of someone in recovery, it's not unusual to feel left out of the relationship that they might have with a buddy. Realising you cannot bond with the addict in the same way, perhaps you might feel a bit miffed about that. But remember the positive aspects of this association and try to let it develop if it's going to be a real boost.

Finding alternatives

Stopping drinking will not immediately solve all the problems you had before you started. If emotional issues are at the root of your problem, those issues will still be there. If you have relationship or marital problems, so too will those. Part of rehabilitation is to tackle those things to help reduce the desire to drink in the future, but don't push yourself too hard. Deal with issues as you feel able, and don't overload yourself; what you're doing is tough and you should feel very proud of yourself for making the hardest decision in the first place – to give up. One thing at a time eh?

Often one of the positive things to come out of quitting is the realisation that actually, it really was just the drinking that was the problem. That might sound like a funny thing to say, but those in denial may have long harboured a belief that something else was wrong – perhaps they thought they were mad; or generally violent; or stupid; or unemployable. Removing the alcohol from your life is like opening the curtains and looking clearly at the room behind you, for the first time in a long time.

This can be a really good time to re-evaluate life. Take stock of where you are, and where you want to be. Suddenly you have choices!

It's a definite factor that the time normally spent drinking is now going to be empty. It's often the case that recovering alcohol abusers fall off the wagon simply through not protecting themselves from recognised weak spots – times of the day when they used to drink, people and places that are associated purely with drinking. There will have been a whole lot of each day taken up with the pastime of drinking, and finding something else to fill that time is important. It's also really important to be prepared. If someone offers you a drink, know in advance what you're going to say.

If you're supporting a recovering alcoholic, get rid of the booze in the house. Apart from removing temptation, it works on many other levels. It shows solidarity and respect too. You don't need it either – tip the stuff down the sink!

This could often be the time of life when people look at new careers or re-training. Very common is for recovered alcoholics to go into support care themselves and become counsellors or buddies – but this could be way down the line when the habit is well under control. Whatever it is, find something to do as soon as you're strong enough, because that ole devil is waiting for you, just looking for an opportunity to knock on the door again. Get busy! And stay out of that pub!

One day at a time

The most important factor in all this is to be realistic. Rome wasn't built in a day, and if you've had a long term or obsessive relationship with alcohol, giving up isn't going to be like clicking your fingers. The biggest part is making the decision, for sure, but the rest of it takes time. Habits are hard to break, and you may have lived your life immersed in alcohol for a long time. So be aware that you need to take one day at a time. If you wake up feeling positive, and go to bed each day without falling by the wayside, you can give yourself a massive pat on the back, because only you will appreciate how hard just doing that is some days.

There are drugs available that replicate the way a certain gene breaks down alcohol in the liver. Some people have it naturally, and the gene causes flushing, nausea and palpitations. Understandably, those people cannot tolerate alcohol. This reaction can be created pharmaceutically and this might be an option if you are seriously worried about being able to say no.

But if you make mistakes and have slip ups, don't lose heart. We all make mistakes, and as long as you can haul yourself back up again, look at it realistically and not let it become the norm once again, it's fine. Each day will make you stronger, and there will come a time when you don't have slip ups and you are strong. At the beginning, just take it one day at a time.

Summing Up

Stay positive and look ahead. Your whole life stretches before you, and taking this step towards a brighter, sober existence can only be a good thing.

There will be days when you feel tempted. Of course there will. And there will be days that you give in. But keep at it – it can only get better.

If you're not the alcoholic, but the carer or supporting family, remember this: it's a huge and frightening step and mistakes will happen. Try not to be angry when it goes a bit wrong and don't rush things, but be around to support, and don't be judgmental. It's really tough and you should be very proud of them. It's also tough on you, of course. But things will be so much better without alcohol around.

Help List

General information

Advice for Alcohol Problems (APAS)

36 Park Row, Nottingham, NG1 6GR
Tel: 0115 948 5570
www.apas.org.uk
APAS is an independent provider of services designed to reduce the harm
alcohol causes to individuals and their families. The website contains lots of
useful information and contacts.

Alcoholics Anonymous

PO Box 1, 10 Toft Green, York, YO1 7ND
National helpline: 0845 769 7555
www.alcoholics-anonymous.org.uk
This is a worldwide organisation offering regular support groups and meetings
for those giving up drinking. Visit the website for more details on how they work
and how to join a group in your area.

Alcohol Concern

Alcohol Concern, 64 Leman Street, London, E1 8EU
Tel: 020 7264 0510
contact@alcoholconcern.org.uk
www.alcoholconcern.org.uk
This is the national voluntary agency dealing with alcohol misuse. It works to
reduce the incidence and costs of alcohol-related harm and to increase the
range and quality of services available to people with alcohol-related problems.
Also offers a services directory for those looking for support groups UK-wide.

Alcohol Focus Scotland

2nd Floor, 166 Buchanan Street, Glasgow, G1 2LW
Tel: 0141 572 6700
enquiries@alcohol-focus-scotland.org.uk
www.alcohol-focus-scotland.org.uk
Scotland's national voluntary organisation offering information and advice about responsible drinking. The website contains a range of downloadable leaflets and provides information and training on alcohol related issues.

British Liver Trust

2 Southampton Road, Ringwood, BH24 1HY
Helpline: 0800 652 7330
General enquiries: 01425 481320
info@britishlivertrust.org.uk
www.britishlivertrust.org.uk
The British Liver Trust promotes education and research around liver health. The website contains information and advice on the causes, signs, symptoms and treatment of liver disease. This is a useful resource for people suffering from liver disease and for those concerned about relatives, friends or colleagues.

Down Your Drink

www.downyourdrink.org.uk
Run by Alcohol Concern, Down Your Drink is for people who are worried about their drinking. You can find out if you are drinking too much and benefit from online support.

The Drink Debate

www.thedrinkdebate.org.uk
This webpage provides facts about drink and a list of useful links.

Drinkline

Tel: 0800 917 8282
Set up by Alcohol Concern, this is a freephone helpline offering either recorded information or the opportunity to talk to an advisor. Help is available to callers worried about their own drinking and support is given to the family and friends of people who are drinking.

Drinksafely

www.liverinfo.org.uk
This looks at all aspects of drinking alcohol. Also includes the 'Drinkulator' traffic light drink calculator, which allows you to check if you're drinking too much.

The Drinkaware Trust

7 - 10 Chandos Street, London, W1G 9DQ
Tel: 020 7307 7450
www.drinkaware.co.uk
This was set up in 2006 by the Portman Group to improve public awareness and understanding of responsible drinking. On the website you'll find useful information about alcohol and drinking, and practical tips and facts to help you become more drink aware. A drink diary is included.

Frank (or Talk to Frank) (Also called National Drugs Helpline)

Helpline: 0800 77 66 00
frank@talktofrank.com
www.talktofrank.com
Talk to Frank is also called The National Drugs Helpline and provides a freephone helpline and website offering advice, information and support, not just to addicts but carers too. Email enquiries through the website.

Health Scotland

Tel: 0131 536 5500
www.healthscotland.com
publications@health.scot.nhs.uk (publication requests)
Health Scotland publishes information leaflets and leads education campaigns on health issues aimed at the Scottish public. Their publications section contains factsheets, leaflets and booklets on a wide range of health issues, including those around alcohol.

Know Your Limits

www.knowyourlimits.gov.uk
This website is aimed at younger drinkers with a hard-hitting, no nonsense approach. Includes role-playing options to highlight dangers of excessive drinking.

National Organisation on Foetal Alcohol Syndrome UK (NOFAS-UK)

157 Beaufort Park, London, NW11 6DA
Tel: 0208 458 5951
Funded Helpline 08700 333 700
nofas-uk@midlantic.co.uk
www.nofas-uk.org
Dedicated to providing support and information for children and families affected by Foetal Alcohol Syndrome.

Patient UK

www.patient.co.uk
Provides information on a wide range of health issues, including alcoholism and problem drinking.

Truth About Booze

The Drinkaware Trust, 7 - 10 Chandos Street, London, W1G 9DQ
Tel: 020 7307 7450
www.truthaboutbooze.com
Part of the Drinkaware Trust, this site is aimed at giving realistic support to younger binge drinkers.

Support for families and professionals

Al-Anon

Head office:
61 Great Dover Street, London, SE1 4YF
Tel: 020 7403 0888 (Helpline 10am - 10pm, 365 days a year)
enquiries@al-anonuk.org.uk
Scotland:
Al-Anon Information Centre, Mansfield Park Building Unit 6, 22 Mansfield Street, Partick, Glasgow G11 5QP
Tel: 0141 339 8884 (Helpline 10am - 10pm, 365 days a year)
Eire:
Al-Anon Information Centre, Room 5, 5 Capel Street, Dublin 1, EIRE

Tel: 00353 01 873 2699 (Helpline 10.30am – 2.30pm, Mon – Fri)
(Outside Eire use the country code 00353 and omit the first 0)
Northern Ireland:
Al-Anon Information Centre, Peace House, 224 Lisburn Road, Belfast, BT9 6GE
Tel: 028 9068 2368 (Helpline 10am – 1pm, Mon – Fri/ 6pm – 11pm, 7 days a week)
www.al-anonuk.org.uk
This organisation offers support groups and meetings for family and friends of
those who are giving up drinking. Al-Anon believe alcoholism is a family illness
and that changed attitudes can aid recovery.

Alateen

Tel: 020 7403 0888

www.al-anonuk.org.uk/alateen

Part of Al-Anon, this organisation offers support to younger family members
(aged 12 to 17) affected by a problem drinker.

Alcohol Education and Research Council (AERC)

Room 178, Queen Anne Business Centre, 28 Broadway, London SW1H 9JX

Tel: 020 7340 9502

www.aerc.org.uk

AERC administers the Alcohol and Education Research Fund, for education
and research on national alcohol-related issues. Email queries through the
website. A useful resource for professionals.

Families Anonymous

Helpline: 0845 120 0660

office@famanon.org.uk

www.famanon.org.uk

A self-help fellowship for the families of drug abusers. Call the helpline to find
out if there is a FA support group in your area.

Includem (Alcohol and Young Women Project)

23 Scotland Street, Glasgow, G5 8ND
Tel: 0141 429 3492
enquiries@includem.co.uk
www.includem.org

Includem works with socially excluded young people, care leavers and young offenders in many areas of Scotland. It covers a wide range of issues, including misuse of alcohol.

Institute of Alcohol Studies

Tel: 01480 466766
www.ias.org.uk
An independent organisation set up to increase awareness of alcohol-related issues in society. The website contains many useful fact sheets.

Kids Health

www.kidshealth.org.
This US online magazine has some useful advice for teenagers. There are articles on how to cope with an alcoholic parent and what to do if you've got an alcohol problem yourself.

Medical Council on Alcohol

www.medicouncilalcol.demon.co.uk/about.htm
A useful resource for professionals, the Medical Council on Alcohol is a charity concerned with the education of the medical and allied professions about the effects of alcohol on our health. There are links to publications and journals and contact details for regional advisors.

Mentor Foundation UK

Mentor Foundation UK, Fourth Floor, 74 Great Eastern Street, London , EC2A 3JG
Tel: +44 20 7739 8494
admin@mentoruk.org
www.mentoruk.org
Mentor UK works to prevent drug-related harm in children and young people. It supports those working with young people to find the best ways to implement effective drug prevention initiatives.

The National Association for Children of Alcoholics (NACOA)

PO Box 64, Fishponds, Bristol, BS16 2UH
Tel: 0117 924 8005
Helpline: 0800 358 3456

www.nacoa.org.uk
This organisation offers support and advice for children of alcoholics, whether
they're young or grown up. Information is also provided for those concerned
about children's welfare.

Parents Against Drug Abuse (PADA)

Helpline: 08457 023867
admin@pada.org.uk
www.btinternet.com/~padahelp

PADA provides support for the parents and families of drug users.

Parentline Plus

520 Highgate Studios, 53-79 Highgate Road, Kentish Town, London, NW5 1TL
Tel: 0808 800 2222
www.parentlineplus.org.uk

This provides a freephone helpline for parents worried about their children's
drinking. The website contains lots of useful information on a wide range of
topics, including alcohol. Also runs parenting courses and provides a list of
further contacts.

The Portman Group

Tel: 020 7907 3700
info@portmangroup.org.uk
www.portman-group.org.uk

Established in 1989, The Portman Group is supported by the UK's leading
drink producers to help promote sensible drinking. Their role is to encourage
and challenge the industry to promote its products responsibly.

The Priory Group

Corporate Communications, Priory Central Office, Priory House, Randalls Way,
Leatherhead, Surrey, KT22 7TP
Tel: 01372 860 400
info@priorygroup.com
www.priorygroup.com

The Priory Group is a leading independent provider of health services, information and research, which includes alcohol-related issues. Their purpose is to work with patients, residents and students to help them take control of their lives and achieve their maximum potential.

Release

388 Old Street, London, EC1V 9LT
Helpline: 0845 450 0215
ask@release.org.uk
www.release.org.uk
Release offers a range of specialist services to professionals and the public concerning drugs, including information on alcohol. They give advice to drug users, their families, friends and statutory and voluntary agencies.

Drug information

Action on Addiction

Head Office: East Knoyle, Wiltshire, SP3 6BE
Tel: 0845 126 4130
www.actiononaddiction.org.uk
Action on Addiction aims to tackle and disarm addiction through research, treatment, family support, education and training. Useful links for treatment and recovery options. Click on the map to find the contact details for each UK site.

Addaction

Head Office: 67-69 Cowcross Street, London, EC1M 6PU
Tel: 0207 251 5860
info@addaction.org.uk
www.addaction.org.uk
UK treatment agency offering support to recovering addicts plus families and communities to cope with the effects of drug and alcohol misuse.

ADFAM (Families, Drugs & Alcohol)

25 Corsham Street, London, N1 6DR
Tel: 020 7553 7640

www.adfam.org.uk

This is a site for families of alcohol and drug users. It offers information and advice, including a list of local family support services. ADFAM provides direct support to families through publications, training, outreach work and signposting to local support services.

Drug Scope

40 Bermondsey Street, London, SE1 3UD
Tel: 020 7940 7500
info@drugscope.org.uk
www.drugscope.org.uk

Drug Scope provides information and resources for professionals and the public on drug-related issues. It provides an online encyclopaedia of drugs and a directory of help sources.

Narcotics Anonymous (NA)

Tel: 0845 373 3366 (Open 10am until 10pm, seven days a week)
www.ukna.org

Information is provided for those who think they may have a drug problem, recovering addicts and professionals working with addicts seeking recovery. Visit the contacts page for details of NA regional offices in the UK and contact numbers for the rest of the world.

National Drugs Helpline (Department of Health)

Also called Talk to Frank
Tel: 0800 77 66 00
frank@talktofrank.com
www.talktofrank.com

The National Drugs Helpline is also called Talk to Frank and provides a freephone helpline. The website offers advice, information and support, not just to addicts but carers too.

Scottish Drugs Forum (SDF)

91 Mitchell Street, Glasgow, G1 3LN
Tel: 0141 221 1175

enquiries@sdf.org.uk

www.sdf.org.uk

This is a drugs policy and information agency co-ordinating effective response to drug use in Scotland. SDF aims to support and represent, at both local and national levels, a wide range of interests, promoting collaborative, evidence-based responses to drug use.

Sexual health

Condom Essential Wear

Helpline: 0800 567 123

www.condomessentialwear.co.uk

This organisation provides you with everything you need to know to stay healthy and protected. A free and confidential helpline is available.

Rape Crisis

info@rapecrisis.org.uk

www.rapecrisis.org.uk

This website provides information for victims of sexual violence, their friends and families. Use the map provided to find details of local rape crisis groups. A comprehensive list of contacts and links is provided.

Need - 2 - Know

Available Titles

Drugs A Parent's Guide
ISBN 978-1-86144-043-3 £8.99

Dyslexia and Other Learning Difficulties
A Parent's Guide ISBN 978-1-86144-042-6 £8.99

Bullying A Parent's Guide
ISBN 978-1-86144-044-0 £8.99

Working Mothers The Essential Guide
ISBN 978-1-86144-048-8 £8.99

Teenage Pregnancy The Essential Guide
ISBN 978-1-86144-046-4 £8.99

How to Pass Exams A Parent's Guide
ISBN 978-1-86144-047-1 £8.99

Child Obesity A Parent's Guide
ISBN 978-1-86144-049-5 £8.99

Sexually Transmitted Infections
The Essential Guide ISBN 978-1-86144-051-8 £8.99

Alcoholism The Family Guide
ISBN 978-1-86144-050-1 £8.99

Divorce and Separation The Essential Guide
ISBN 978-1-86144-053-2 £8.99

Applying to University The Essential Guide
ISBN 978-1-86144-052-5 £8.99

ADHD The Essential Guide
ISBN 978-1-86144-060-0 £8.99

Student Cookbook - Healthy Eating The Essential Guide
ISBN 978-1-86144-061-7 £8.99

Stress The Essential Guide
ISBN 978-1-86144-054-9 £8.99

Single Parents The Essential Guide
ISBN 978-1-86144-055-6 £8.99

Adoption and Fostering A Parent's Guide
ISBN 978-1-86144-056-3 £8.99

Special Educational Needs A Parent's Guide
ISBN 978-1-86144-057-0 £8.99

The Pill An Essential Guide
ISBN 978-1-86144-058-7 £8.99

Diabetes The Essential Guide
ISBN 978-1-86144-059-4 £8.99

To order our titles, please give us a call on **01733 898103**,
email **sales@n2kbooks.com**, or visit **www.need2knowbooks.co.uk**

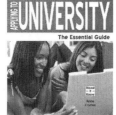
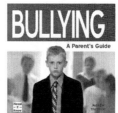

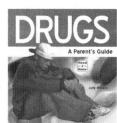

Need - 2 - Know, Remus House, Coltsfoot Drive, Peterborough, PE2 9JX